The Confederation Poets

The Founding Of A Canadian Poetry, 1880 To The First World War

Essential Essays 79

Canada Council for the Arts / Conseil des Arts du Canada

ONTARIO ARTS COUNCIL
CONSEIL DES ARTS DE L'ONTARIO
an Ontario government agency
un organisme du gouvernement de l'Ontario

Canada

Guernica Editions Inc. acknowledges the support of the Canada Council for the Arts and the Ontario Arts Council. The Ontario Arts Council is an agency of the Government of Ontario.

We acknowledge the financial support of the Government of Canada.

The Confederation Poets

The Founding Of A Canadian Poetry,
1880 To The First World War

JAMES DEAHL

GUERNICA
EDITIONS
TORONTO • CHICAGO • BUFFALO • LANCASTER (U.K.)
2022

Guernica Founder: Antonio D'Alfonso

Michael Mirolla, general editor
Julie Roorda, editor
Cover and Interior Design: David Moratto
Guernica Editions Inc.
287 Templemead Drive, Hamilton (ON), Canada L8W 2W4
2250 Military Road, Tonawanda, N.Y. 14150-6000 U.S.A.
www.guernicaeditions.com

Distributors:
Independent Publishers Group (IPG)
600 North Pulaski Road, Chicago IL 60624
University of Toronto Press Distribution (UTP)
5201 Dufferin Street, Toronto (ON), Canada M3H 5T8
Gazelle Book Services, White Cross Mills
High Town, Lancaster LA1 4XS U.K.

First edition.
Printed in Canada.

Legal Deposit—Third Quarter
Library of Congress Catalog Card Number: 2022934711
Library and Archives Canada Cataloguing in Publication
Title: The confederation poets : the founding of a Canadian poetry, 1880 to the First World War / James Deahl.
Names: Deahl, James, 1945- author.
Series: Essential essays series ; 79.
Description: Series statement: Essential essays series ; 79
Identifiers: Canadiana (print) 20220202842 | Canadiana (ebook) 20220202958 | ISBN 9781771837477 (softcover) | ISBN 9781771837484 (EPUB)
Subjects: LCSH: Canadian poetry—19th century—History and criticism. | LCSH: Canadian poetry—20th century—History and criticism. | CSH: Canadian poetry (English)—20th century—History and criticism.
Classification: LCC PS8151 .C63 2022 | DDC C811/.409—dc23

Dedicated to
my friend
Raymond Souster
People's Poet,
Publisher,
& Editor.

No poet did more
for our Confederation Poets,
for Canada,
and for poetry that
celebrates Canada.

Ultimately, we are what we are because we are where we are.
It was the first task for the Canadian imagination to possess the land.

—Malcolm Ross

CONTENTS

Author's Introduction:
The Tory In Every Woodlot

Red Toryism[1] is a political movement that draws inspiration from the writings of English theologian Richard Hooker.[2] It found its first major political expression in the government of British Prime Minister Benjamin Disraeli.[3] Canada, being a colony of England, imported a measure of this Red Tory tradition. Indeed, the first Canadian Prime Minister, Sir John A. Macdonald,[4] is sometimes considered to have been a Red Tory. Be that as it may, Red Toryism in Canada, to the extent that it fully existed or developed, differed from its English cousin. By the time Disraeli died in 1881, the Tories of England were decidedly Blue.

In broad terms, as I use it here, Canadian Red Tories supported both the British Empire and the Crown. Their goal was a united and independent Canada as *part of* the Empire and under the Monarchy. They did not seek the total independence of the U.S. model. They also rejected the rugged individualism popular in the lower part of North America. Rather, our Red Tories supported community-strengthening programs. They saw Canada, not as a collection of free-acting individuals, each striving to advance his/her own ends, but as a *social* community in which people could rely on and support each other. And they rejected, for the most part, the rigid class stratification of the Blue Tories in England.

In British North America, this Canadian version has its roots in the Confederation Period (from the 1860s to the turn of the century). It is of signal importance to note that political movements do not create cultures. Rather, cultures give rise to ideologies, and ideologies yield political movements. There had to exist a *culture* of Red Toryism among the people—by this I mean the broader population, not just the intellectual class—of 19th century Canada for anything else to follow. This popular culture provided the soil for a political movement that, among other things, led to the creation of Canada as a nation state.[5] To understand what Canada was, as well as what it might have become, one must understand the popular culture of the time, especially as displayed by the Poets of the Confederation Period.[6]

I have selected the following poets for this study: George Frederick Cameron, Wilfred Campbell, Bliss Carman, Helena Coleman, Isabella Valancy Crawford, Susan Frances Harrison, Sophia M. Almon Hensley, John Frederic Herbin, E. Pauline Johnson, Archibald Lampman, William Douw Lighthall, Sir Charles G.D. Roberts, Duncan Campbell Scott, Frederick George Scott, Barry Straton, and Ethelwyn Wetherald. All of them were born between 1850 and Confederation in 1867. They have been chosen based on (1) the quality of their poetry, (2) their importance to readers in their own time, and (3) their contribution to the establishment of a CanLit canon. Although many of these poets also wrote prose fiction, prose non-fiction, and drama, they are presented here as poets. Some like Lampman are major figures today, others like Cameron have been largely forgotten, but every one of them produced fine verse that can be read and enjoyed today.

I do not suggest that these poets formed a cabal. There is little to connect Isabella Valancy Crawford with Sir Charles G.D. Roberts; there is little to connect Pauline Johnson with Archibald Lampman. What these poets do connect with is the general culture of their era. While individual poets as well as others in the arts do not create a culture (although some poets might think they do), they can weigh and refine their culture and eventually give it voice. Like other citizens, poets are *part of* a culture. They may embrace it; they may reject it. They may even help extend and articulate that culture. But, whatever their personal stance, they all arise from it. In the case of these Confederation Poets, they were from the Red Tory culture that formed the early Canada during the concluding decades of the 19th century.

It is not the intention of this study to argue for or against the Red Tory *bona fides* of Sir John A. Macdonald or John Diefenbaker,[7] in whom the movement may have found its final echo almost a hundred years later during the early 1960s. This paper seeks to direct its reader to the actual work of the writers of late 19th century Canada, to their books and essays. These writers are essential to developing any understanding of Canada, then or at present. In *The New Oxford Book of Canadian Verse in English*, used in many colleges and universities as a standard text, Margaret Atwood presents a small taste of this poetry. She has chosen four poems by Isabella Valancy Crawford, six by Sir Charles G.D. Roberts, six by Archibald Lampman, four by Wilfred Campbell, three by Bliss Carman, only one by Frederick George Scott, five by Duncan Campbell Scott, and only two by E. Pauline Johnson. Atwood's choices are excellent, as one might expect. And, except for Frederick George Scott and Pauline Johnson, these poets are not seriously underrepresented, given the nature of this type of survey anthology. However, it is deeply unfortunate that Atwood offers no poems at all by George Frederick Cameron, Helena Coleman, Susan Frances Harrison, Sophia M. Almon Hensley, John Frederic Herbin, William Douw Lighthall, and Ethelwyn Wetherald. Readers of *The New Oxford Book of Canadian Verse in English* do not have nearly enough works from the Confederation Period to understand the ethos these poets were reflecting or writing from. And beyond anthologies like Atwood's, how easy is it to find enough poems to form a true opinion? Not easy at all.[8]

Upon close examination, it turns out that a hundred and fifty years ago, Red Tories played a strong role in society. In one way or another, the poets mentioned above confronted the problem of how to strike the best balance between the duty a free people have to their community, be it their local village or their country as a whole, and the desires of every individual for self-expression and to defend his/her self-interest. In socialism, there might be too much communal duty, the individual could be stifled; in American capitalism, there might be too great a veneration of the rugged individual at the expense of a just society. Neither would be the Canadian way, at least not back then. (Today might be a different story.) The political implications of this conflict between the individual and society as thinkers struggled to discover the best road to the common good is among the topics examined by William Christian and Colin Campbell in their *Political Parties and Ideologies in Canada: Liberals, Conservatives, Socialists, Nationalists.*[9]

This is not to suggest that the Poets of Confederation were primarily fixated on politics. They were not. But they were concerned for their new nation and about the direction it would take in the world. As Christian people, they were also concerned with the morally correct way to live a life. The scope of this book precludes a full discussion of the poets studied, but at the risk of reducing these complex writers to a few highlights, something brief must be said about each of them.

Sir Charles G.D. Roberts is considered by some to be the Father of Canadian Literature because *Orion, and Other Poems* along with his other early books inspired so many of his fellow writers. Conflict features in the writings of Sir Charles: the conflict between wilderness and civilization, especially as experienced in the small fishing and farming villages in his native New Brunswick, as well as in the backwoods regions, including the rugged wilderness of its interior. In this he seeks a balance between the land and the needs (or desires) of the people. As Canada became ever more urban, ever more industrial, all that existed of the "real" Canada was often consigned to memory, and to poetry, where it would be preserved against change, at least for a few decades.

Isabella Valancy Crawford was often concerned with conflict, with the struggle between good and evil, between beauty and ugliness, and ultimately, between life and death. She saw redemption through suffering, and these struggles often happened in the backwoods areas of Ontario. Her formative years were spent in Paisley, Canada West (as Ontario was known then). In those days that was truly pioneer territory. Crawford then moved to Lakefield, not exactly an urban area back in her time. She would die in poverty in Toronto.

Crawford was patriotic, and the hardships suffered by individuals, both urban and rural, often informed her work. Another important dimension of her writing was her inclusion of Aboriginal tales and myths, most unusual for a woman of her day.

Frederick George Scott was another religious poet. He was a strong Anglo-Catholic who served as rector of St. Matthew's Church, was later a canon, and finally became an archdeacon. Like Wilfred Campbell, he also viewed the Monarchy and the Empire as essential to the Canadian tradition, institutions that would help prevent Canada from being absorbed into the United States. In this way Scott was a firm Red Tory who wanted a vital and compassionate Canada under the British Crown. His poetry is generally concerned with death, the crisis of religious faith in a secular world, and the survival of the natural world, especially the Laurentian region of his native Québec. One could consider Scott to be a late-Victorian poet with a markedly Canadian flavour in both his religious verse and in his renderings of the natural landscape. Having been born in Montréal and having died in Québec City, Scott was the foremost English-language poet from 19th century Québec.

George Frederick Cameron was, from shortly after his death into the early part of the 20th century, considered to be among the finest poets of his period. During his life, however, he was largely unknown. Cameron died at age thirty of heart disease. Had it not been for his brother, Charles J. Cameron, our poet would not be part of the story of Canada. Fortunately, two years following George Frederick Cameron's death in 1885, his brother brought out *Lyrics on Freedom, Love and Death*. As early as 1881—four years prior to the publication of Cameron's book—Archibald Lampman ranked him alongside Sir Charles G.D. Roberts, and thirty-two years later Wilfred Campbell included five of Cameron's poems in the 1913 edition of *The Oxford Book of Canadian Verse*. Cameron was a serious Christian and classical thinker who continued Charles Sangster's themes of love, truth, and beauty. His posthumous poetry collection contributed to the making of Canada during the years following Confederation.

William Douw Lighthall, unlike Cameron, enjoyed a long life. He was born in 1857, before most of his fellow Confederation Poets, and he lived until 1954, becoming the last of our poets to die. Nonetheless, Lighthall only published two volumes of poetry, and those thirty-five years apart. Because of an anthology he edited, *Songs of the Great Dominion: Voices from the Forests and Waters, the Settlements and Cities of Canada*,[10] he greatly influenced the direction of Canadian poetry. This was the first anthology to include the verse of Confederation Poets such as George Frederick Cameron, Wilfred Campbell, Bliss Carman, Isabella Valancy Crawford, Susan Frances Harrison, E. Pauline Johnson, Archibald Lampman, Charles G.D. Roberts, Duncan Campbell Scott, and Frederick George Scott. *Songs of the Great Dominion* set the stage for the publication of Wilfred Campbell's *The Oxford Book of Canadian Verse* in 1913 because Campbell often followed Lighthall's lead. Lighthall was another important poet based in Québec.

Archibald Lampman was born in Morpeth, Canada West—yet another poet located far from the urban centres of the new Dominion. Like the young Sir Charles G.D. Roberts in the Bay of Fundy area, Lampman was a wilderness enthusiast, albeit the wilderness of central Canada, for he spent his adult life in Ottawa. He also was concerned with the conflict between the natural world and modern civilization, to a degree reminiscent of William Blake's struggle between innocence and experience, with the Canadian wilderness viewed as a kind of innocence and the city representing the experience of avarice and a land despoiled. Lampman's great poem, "The City of the End of Things,"[11] clearly sums up his thought on what Canada was becoming. It is both observation and warning. Lampman also was concerned, perhaps *distressed*, with the battle between human desire and the moral life demanded by his Anglican upbringing. (His father was of the clergy.) Archibald Lampman, Wilfred Campbell, and Duncan Campbell Scott wrote a column for *The Globe* (now *The Globe and Mail*) newspaper called "At the Mermaid Inn." In this way these three Confederation Poets became public intellectuals.

Wilfred Campbell, like Archibald Lampman, was the son of an Anglican clergyman. Campbell was born in Berlin, Canada West (now Kitchener, Ontario), and later attended secondary school in Owen Sound. This is not too far from Paisley, where Isabella Valancy Crawford spent her early years. In his days as in hers it was truly backwoods Ontario. Campbell, like the others in this study, was concerned with the conflict between the old Canada of small towns, strong families, and religious faith versus the new cities, the questions about nature and natural order raised by scientism, and the secularization of urban life. Because of his strong Christian faith Campbell became an ordained Episcopal minister (although he later resigned his ministry), and because of his belief that the Monarchy could provide an anchor for a society drifting towards chaos, he was perhaps the strongest Red Tory of the poets we are discussing. (Unfortunately, his world would reach chaos during the summer of 1914 with the outbreak of the War to End All Wars.)

Sophia M. Almon Hensley is the youngest poet included in this study. She was born in 1866, just one year prior to Confederation. More than any other poet in this group, Hensley was a poet of romantic love, and she celebrated the joys and sorrows of the heart. She was a protégé of Sir Charles G.D. Roberts and the subject of some of the older poet's love poetry. (Their relationship was a possible cause of the breakup of Roberts' marriage in 1897.) A world traveller and a free spirit, Hensley was educated in England and Paris, and lived for much of her life in New York, England, and on the British Channel Islands, although she frequently visited her native Nova Scotia. In fact, she counted St. Marys Bay as one of her best-loved spots.

John Frederic Herbin is unique among the English-language writers of the Confederation Period in that he was an Acadian. His mother was Marie-Marguerite Robichaud, and although Herbin identified strongly with her and the Acadian People, he chose English. (His father, John Herbin, was a Huguenot who came to Canada from Cambrai, France.) Herbin's main topic was the Acadian Diaspora (1755–1763). He spent his adult life in Wolfville,

Nova Scotia, not far from the old Acadian village of Grand-Pré, a landscape later made famous by Bliss Carman in his first book. Like George Frederick Cameron, John Frederic Herbin was also given national prominence by Archibald Lampman, who did much to promote his fellow poets. Were it not for Herbin, there would be little in Canadian literature about the Acadian People and their suffering.

Susan Frances Harrison, who often used the *nom de plume* Seranus, was one of three Confederation women included in Lighthall's landmark collection *Songs of the Great Dominion*. Unlike Crawford and Johnson, Harrison studied for a couple of years in Montréal and developed a keen interest in Québécois literature. The title of her début collection of verse, *Pine, Rose, and Fleur de Lis*, shows her attachment to the landscape, history, and themes of both Ontario and Québec, rare for a writer based in Toronto. She was the most widely read woman writer of prose and poetry of her generation and, unlike many other Confederation women, is still read today, if only by scholars. Because Harrison was also a journalist—she wrote for *The Globe* (forerunner of *The Globe and Mail*), the (Detroit) *Free Press*, and *The Week*, where she briefly served as editor—her work is valued by students of the period.

Bliss Carman is often called Canada's first People's Poet. (He especially inspired Al Purdy, one of the giants of 20th century poetry.) Raised as an Anglican, Carman later became a pantheist and a *mystical* Romantic. His is often a poetry of longing and loss, a poetry balanced between a past he cannot hold and a future of uncertain values. Above all, Carman strove to embrace an optimism of his own making in the face of change. Through poetry he thought he could meld the mundane realm of human affairs with the divine realm of the spirit. Unlike many other Transcendentalists, Carman's thought lacks intellectual rigour and his poetry is more concerned with emotions than ideas. Perhaps because of this, he was extremely popular in both the United States and Canada. Like his colleagues, Carman was concerned about the future Canada was to enter with the turn of the century.

Duncan Campbell Scott was also the son of a minister; in Scott's case his family was Methodist. Although born in Ottawa, he was schooled in Smiths Falls, at that time quite a small place. His employment in the Indian Branch of the Canadian government (now Indigenous Affairs and Northern Development Canada) brought him into contact with the Indigenous Peoples and with the more remote regions of Ontario, including James Bay. As with some other writers covered here, Scott was deeply concerned about the conflict between the natural Canadian landscape and the Indigenous Peoples who lived there and the culture of Britain and Western Europe, imported by the colonists. Then, as now, the struggle of the First Nations communities was one of raw survival, both cultural and all too often physical. Featured in Scott's poetry is the conflict between the religions of the Indigenous Canadians and the Christian teaching of the missionaries. This spiritual struggle had its sharpest example in Canada's Residential Schools, which Scott administrated for several years. In addition to the religious conflict, Scott's body of work includes the struggle between the simple village life he knew as a child and the modern forces of industrialization and urbanization.

E. Pauline Johnson was a Mohawk born on the Six Nations reserve near Brantford, Canada West. She was, however, educated in the tradition of British literature and history. (This was largely due to her mother, Emily Susanna Howells.) Johnson also knew the history and culture, especially the traditional legends, of the Mohawk people. Like Bliss Carman, Johnson was extremely popular in both the United States and Canada. As might be expected, she wrote about the conflict between the traditional life she knew from birth and the new Canada powered by Western European values and technologies. As a Native woman, she was both a Canadian and a Six Nations patriot, and also provided a public voice for the Aboriginal People. She thought the resiliency of the "British connection" would serve as a buffer to help preserve Canada from becoming totally Americanized.[12] This was a common belief during the Confederation Period. Like the other writers mentioned here,

Johnson was part of the great Romantic tradition. It was the culture of the time.

Ethelwyn Wetherald, like all of our poets discussed here, was a Christian. She is, however, the only Quaker in the group. Her father was the Reverend William Wetherald, founder of the Rockwood Academy. Our young poet studied under her father, and later attended the Friends' Boarding School in Union Springs, New York. She returned to Canada to become a writer. While Wetherald addressed many topics, she is remembered for her nature poetry. She was so well known, in fact, that when her *The Last Robin: Lyrics and Sonnets* appeared in 1907, Earl Grey, then Governor General of Canada, purchased twenty-five copies to give to his friends. As is common among our poets of nature, such as Archibald Lampman, Sir Charles G.D. Roberts, and Wilfred Campbell, Wetherald was concerned with the tension between the natural beauty of Canada and the spreading urban and industrial areas, like Toronto and Hamilton. She chose nature.

Helena Coleman, like Ethelwyn Wetherald, occupies a unique position. Unlike all other important writers, both of poetry and fiction, from the Confederation Period, Coleman did not publish her initial poetry collection until the 20th century. Coleman was born in Ontario in 1860 (the same year as Sir Charles G.D. Roberts and John Frederic Herbin, and a year prior to the major quartet of Pauline Johnson, Frederick George Scott, Bliss Carman, and Archibald Lampman), but she did not make her début until 1906, halfway through her fifth decade, and did not publish her important second book until 1917 when she was three years shy of age sixty. Of the poets in the present study, the Pre-Confederation Charles Sangster is a man rooted solidly in the early Romantic Period of Wordsworth and Coleridge. Coleman's fellow Confederation Poets are members of the Victorian Period of Tennyson, Matthew Arnold, and the two Brownings. That is, the Confederation writers are *later* Romantics. But Helena Coleman stands alone as an Edwardian Poet of the era of Thomas Hardy and John Masefield.[13] In this way,

Coleman can be viewed as a bridge between Canada's 19th and 20th centuries, and her masterwork focuses on the First World War.

What these poets of the Confederation Period did, above all else, was discover the real Canada. Prior to the arrival of their books in the 1880s and 1890s, Canada was too often viewed through the lens of British colonial attitudes, and not as a place in its own right. Their vital contribution was to delineate what Canada was, and what it might become, through the twin lenses of her wilderness, quite unlike Britain, and the history and culture of the Indigenous Peoples, which were important for poets like Isabella Valancy Crawford, Pauline Johnson, and Duncan Campbell Scott. One highlight of the books of these poets is their vivid nature poetry. In this they preceded Tom Thomson and the Group of Seven[14] by a generation. It is quite likely that these painters of the early 20th century were introduced to the Canadian wilderness that became their most notable subject by reading the poems of the Confederation Poets, be it the Northern Ontario poems of Duncan Campbell Scott, the Algonquin Park area and Ottawa River valley as celebrated in the verse of Archibald Lampman, Frederick George Scott's Laurentians, or the forest depths of Sir Charles G.D. Roberts' New Brunswick.

The Red Tory tradition in Canada (but not in England, where it has its roots in the thought of the 16th century theologian Richard Hooker) is a child of the Romantic Period. Romantic poetry in English starts with Wordsworth and Blake, runs through Keats and Shelley, achieves a high point in Tennyson, and provides its final echo in the Georgian Poets of the early 20th century. Red Tories attempted to maintain traditional social, economic, and religious values in the face of the onrushing modern era by striking a balance between the past and the future. They were wary of change and of the breakdown of family ties and religious faith, yet understood that while change could not be avoided, it could be managed in a socially responsible manner. Some were nostalgic while others were progressive, but one way or another, they were defeated. Their poetry is seldom taught in schools today. It is nonetheless crucial to savour their vision and to appreciate the nature of their struggle.

Such truncated comments fail to do justice to these complex and varied writers who defined our Confederation Period. The role of these men and women in Canadian culture truly calls for a book longer than this one. (And for the actual reading of *their* books, not merely existing commentary on their poetry, like the present study.[15]) But in general, they share Blake's concern for the tension between innocence and experience. On the one hand there is Canada—the real Canada—as she existed before the unwelcome encroachment of European colonization. On the other hand there is the new Canada that followed the often brutal marginalization of the Native Peoples, the ever-spreading urbanization, and rapid industrialization. This was Canada as she came to be used and exploited by imperial powers, first England, and later the United States, and in the 21st century by powerful Asian and South American interests. The concern of the society at their time was to balance these two Canadas. The result was the development of a Canadian version of Red Toryism, now obscured by Modernism and Postmodernism.

For a series of reasons—some unavoidable—Canadian Red Toryism, which lasted from Macdonald to Diefenbaker, failed. Aside from scattered pockets in Atlantic Canada, no Red Tories survive, not even in their former stronghold of rural Southwestern Ontario, where it could have been said then, as it can no longer be said today, that there was a Tory in every woodlot, a church in every hamlet, and a well-read Bible in every parlour. However, no complete understanding of Canadian culture can exist without an understanding of, and a deep appreciation for, the work of the Poets of Confederation. They were the first to grant clear utterance to the Canadian Dream. The foundation of Canada as we know it lies in the 1880s when their initial books were published. The concerns society harboured then should be our concerns today.

Charles Sangster
Pre-Confederation Mystic

Although he published his famous poetry collection in 1856, before all but three of the Confederation Poets were born, and came from a different era, Charles Sangster built the foundation they were to use a generation later. Sangster's life was almost entirely Ontario-bound. He was born in Kingston on July 16, 1822 in the days when Ontario was still Upper Canada. The poet's father died when the boy was not even two years old, so he retained no memory of his father. Growing up in poverty, Sangster was forced to leave school at age fifteen to help support his widowed mother and his siblings. As a result, he was largely self-educated. Nonetheless, he worked briefly in Amherstburg, where he served as the editor of the *Amherstburg Courier*. Then it was back to Kingston and a position as a reporter for the *Daily News*. Eventually, he made his way to Ottawa, where he put in eighteen years at the Post Office Department, working for a spell with the younger poet Archibald Lampman. And finally he returned to Kingston, where he died on December 9, 1893.

On the surface, his was a rather ordinary life. Many young men of little formal education could be found in the Canada of his time, for university tended to be a middle-class privilege. For most working-class Canadians, to be educated was to be self-educated. It was, however, Sangster's spiritual life of the imagination that was extraordinary. In "The St. Lawrence and the Saguenay"[1] he took a real/metaphysical trip from the city of his birth, through the Thousand Islands, past Montréal, and along the St. Lawrence River to Lévis/Québec City, where, as Milton Acorn reminds us, the current meets the tide.[2] After Québec City one enters the "Atlantic" portion of Québec, quite apart from its inland region of the river's lowlands.

Then, his journey took him into salt water and on eastward to the Gulf of St. Lawrence. Finally, Sangster turned northwest and up the Saguenay River to the magic land of Lac Saint-Jean[3] in the Laurentian Highlands, a realm of unfallen nature.[4] He saw the Saguenay/Lac Saint-Jean region as a sort of Canadian Arcadia.

The quality of Sangster's verse, and his celebration of Canada's natural beauty, can be judged by a few stanzas from "The St. Lawrence and the Saguenay." Here we have the Thousand Islands of the St. Lawrence River in Ontario (stanza IV):[5]

And bathe the vessel's prow. Isle after isle
Is passed, as we glide tortuously through
The opening vistas, that uprise and smile
Upon us from the ever-changing view.
Here nature, lavish of her wealth, did strew
Her flocks of panting islets on the breast
Of the admiring River, where they grew,
Like shapes of Beauty, formed to give a zest
To the charmed mind, like waking Visions of the Blest.

Sangster's journey continues, and here is a stanza set on the river between Montréal and Québec City (stanza XLIV):[6]

Yet there are graceful landscapes thickly strewn
Along these banks, to muse on and admire;
Here stands a maiden cottage all alone,
There the low church extends its gleaming spire.—
Scenes, where Arcadian dreamers might retire,
And live in pastoral meditation, free
From every low, inordinate desire.
Yon group of dwellings—what felicity
Speaks from their eloquent repose! where even he …

Finally, the poet sails up the Saguenay River, through the lands of the Têtes-de-Boule/Atikamekw, towards his goal (stanza LXXXV):[7]

> But they are there, though man may never know
> Their number or their beauty. Pass the eye
> Along the ever-looming scene, where'er we go,
> Through these long corridors of rock and sky—
> What startling barriers, rising sullenly
> From the dark deeps, like giants, seem to place
> An adamantine gateway, close and high,
> To bar our progress; meet them face to face,
> The magic doors fly open, and the rocks recede apace.

While it has been reported that in 1853—three years before his poem was published—the poet took a steamship excursion down the St. Lawrence River and up the Saguenay, the voyage in the book is as much poetic as actual. His literary voyage is not only one of geography, it is also one of time. The poem travels through the Ontario of Sangster's own era into an earlier Québec of the French explorers, and even into his imagined mythology of Indigenous people such as the Algonquin, Innu, and Têtes-de-Boule/Atikamekw tribes.[8] And the time Sangster deals with is both historical time and spiritual time. For this poet, Canada's physical geography is both present and eternal.[9] While Sangster became better known for poems like his much-anthologized patriotic tribute pieces to General Isaac Brock, "From Queenston Heights" and a later poem simply called "Brock," the work which commands our attention today is a longish poem of over fifty pages (110 stanzas with nine lyric poems scattered throughout), written in nine-line Spenserian stanzas, set on the St. Lawrence and Saguenay Rivers. In "The St. Lawrence and the Saguenay" the poet clearly sets out to be our national poet. In my opinion, we should consider Charles Sangster to be our first People's Poet, even though the term was not in common use until almost a century later. As Cornell University's E.K. Brown wrote: "Sangster wrote for his fellow-Canadians, and about them and with a Canadian or, at the widest, a North American range of attitude."[10] He was the first Canadian poet to do so.

Like John Keats before him, who observed that "Beauty is truth,

truth beauty,"[11] our poet states: "I worship Truth and Beauty in my soul."[12] Sangster has one foot in the Bible and his message is, at base, a classic Christian one, while his other foot is planted in the 19th century Romanticism of Wordsworth and Keats. He finds the Biblical God revealed in the natural beauty of Canada, a natural beauty that also informed the spirituality of the Indigenous Peoples. In this way, Sangster's Christianity is at once mystical and romantic.[13] Our poet also finds that human, romantic love is a reflection, or extension, of the Divine love that flows to us from Heaven. By looking for Truth, Beauty, and Love, one can find God, especially if the seeker has a pure heart. The simplicity of rural living, rather than the accelerated pace of an urban life, aids greatly in the search for spiritual truth. One should also avoid doubts that can shake, even destroy, religious faith. And such doubts were becoming increasingly common by the mid-1800s.

But the vision behind "The St. Lawrence and the Saguenay" becomes more complex when the poet references the ancient Greek myth of Arcadia.[14] Sangster tells us that in this part of Canada one can find "Scenes, where Arcadian dreamers might retire,/ And live in pastoral meditation, free/ From every low, inordinate desire."[15] Thus, the Canadian wilderness can be viewed as a sort of unfallen, or redeemed, Eden because there might be a redemptive value, or spirituality, in unspoiled nature. This is especially true of the Canadian Shield region of Ontario and Québec.[16]

While Sangster does not actually claim that the Kingdom of Saguenay (a term he never uses in his poem) and the utopian Arcadia of the Greeks are one and the same, he does describe Lac Saint-Jean in Arcadian terms. And he does more than that; he sees it as a realm where Christian truth is revealed.[17] His poem can be divided into four sections:

1. The St. Lawrence River in Ontario (the Thousand Islands, etc.) from Kingston to just east of Cornwall;
2. The St. Lawrence River in Québec from the Ottawa River to Lévis/Québec City, including Lac Saint-Pierre;

> 3. The estuary of the St. Lawrence River/Gulf of St. Lawrence (the *north* shore thereof) to the Saguenay River;
> 4. The mouth of the Saguenay River at Tadoussac to the realm of the mystical Saguenay/Lac Saint-Jean, supposed site of the Kingdom of Saguenay that Jacques Cartier attempted to find in 1535.

Each segment has its own geography, history, culture, and spiritual essence. On this journey, Sangster deals with English-Canadian, French-Canadian, and Indigenous-Canadian realities, although his chief focus is on the French-Canadian culture of the early days. These are Canada's three founding peoples and all three are valid and necessary to the very idea of Canada. Whatever the poet's failings in terms of style—while he may not have been a great poet, he did write many very good pieces—"The St. Lawrence and the Saguenay" is a serious attempt at a Canadian national myth. The poem's focus is the historic "original nation" of Upper and Lower Canada, that is, of Ontario and Québec.

In seeking a myth to explain the spirit of Canada, Sangster looked east to the old Québec of Habitant culture, and farther east into the past of Jacques Cartier and the first settlers, and then north to the Indigenous Peoples of the Laurentian Highlands region[18] of the Canadian Shield. The Saguenay is depicted as a realm of a stern and harsh, but good, beauty. The poet is awestruck by this raw, unspoiled land. This could be where a real utopia might be located. By the close of his poem, Sangster has a transcendent experience of God. At Trinity Bay, Sangster finds God's Mercy and "sweet felicity." Of the "Godlike Eloquence" of his vision, the poet can speak nothing—it is beyond human words—it is "like Truth made manifest" and his frail voice cannot express it fully. Sangster has both a mystical *and* a romantic Christian vision of the Canadian wilderness. Of the poet's direct experience of God in the Saguenay, David Latham of the University of Lethbridge has written that Sangster's quest is "a journey away from civilization towards nature and the divine creator. ... But as the voyage nears the poet's source of inspiration (symbolized by the river's divine origin), he grows weary of art, which cannot compete with the splendour of God's work, and humbly concludes that the expressive calm of silence in the northern wilderness is a 'Godlike eloquence'."[19] This complex vision is based on Christian theology, Greek myth, and his understanding of Indigenous lore.

It is clear that "The St. Lawrence and the Saguenay" works on several levels, and this makes for a creative tension and an ever-deepening experience in Sangster's best poetry. This ever-deepening experience is at first Sangster's during the composition of his poem, and later his readers share this same experience. As Don Conway of the University of New Brunswick argues: "The tension in Sangster's poetry arises, not from a clash between objective reality and fanciful illusion, but from a dialectic between the real universe as a manifestation of a higher world which makes it significant and the imagination's world which is more personally spiritual."[20] The religious/spiritual content in this poem was also noted by the University of Ottawa's Frank M. Tierney: "The poem is also a journey away from civilization into nature and toward God as revealed in nature." The poet travels down "the St Lawrence, symbolic of the material world, and up the Saguenay, which represents the spiritual life, to ultimate union with each other and with God."[21] What truly concerns Sangster is the relationship between himself and God, the relationship between God and Canada, and the role Canada is to play in God's plan for humanity.

In addition to its spiritual dimension, this fifty-two-page poem has many stunning passages describing the natural attractions of Canada. Sangster believed that when he was in a city such as Ottawa or Kingston, he was in a world made by man. But when he was in the forest, he was in a world made by God. And he set about to show the beauty of God's world. He wrote several longish poems about spring, summer, and autumn, often in a style reminiscent of Keats. He also wrote in a style more his own, such as "The Indian Summer."[22]

The Indian Summer

It is not like the Spring-time, bright
    With budding leaves and opening flowers,
But there's a glory in its light,
Softer than that which falls by night
    On lovers' bowers.
There is a mellow tint on every tree,
And nature's breath is sweet, and all is harmony.

It is not like the Summer time,
    Enlivened by a brilliant sun,
It savors of a purer clime
Than Summer, in its earliest prime,
    E'er smiled upon.
There is a light serene on everything,
Half veiled, and blushing, like a Bride in Spring.

Thou com'st in Autumn, when the trees
    Have doff'd their florid livery,
Ere Winter sweeps, with blighting breeze,
And fetters strong, to bind the seas—
    All hail to thee!
To thee, whose subtle charms no pen can trace,
To whom the artist's skill imparts no flattering grace.

Like almost every other Canadian poet of the 19th century, Sangster wrote beautiful poems describing the Canadian landscape. In the words of Marlene Alt, "His poetry distinguishes him as a lover and keen observer of the natural world. ... Whatever his mood he is consistently and intensely serious and deeply religious."[23] At least in this regard, almost all of the Confederation Poets followed his lead in their own nature poetry. (Even though many of our poets lived in cities like Ottawa, Kingston, Montréal, and Toronto, Canadian poets did not produce high-quality urban poetry until well into the

20th century and the advent of Modernism.) Another example of Sangster's nature poetry, and of his rigid avoidance of cities, is "Canzonet,"[24] one of the short lyrics embedded in "The St. Lawrence and the Saguenay." The site of this love poem is the St. Lawrence River at Montréal Island. In it Sangster has robins, roses, green trees, happy woodlands, and bird-song, yet the city of Montréal is not described. It is not even mentioned. The poem could, for all readers know, take place in a much less urban section of the river.

Canzonet

The balmy summer days are here,
  The Robin warbleth in the tree,
But Summer, Spring, nor song-birds bring
  One note of love from thee.

The roses will put forth their buds,
  Green leaves adorn each ardent tree,
But in my heart will never start
  One rose-bud hope for thee.

The sun leans down to kiss the flowers,
  To flush the blossoms of the tree,
But to my love no carrier-dove
  Brings warmth and light from thee.

The happy woodlands throb with song,
  Music is breathed from tree to tree;
With Winter's fleece these songs will cease,
  But not my love for thee.

Later on, Sangster included Norse material in poems like "A Northern Rune."[25] Here he picks up on the Hyperborean myth, which goes back to the Greek of Herodotus (about 450 B.C.). In Sangster's poem, the Norse King, stout and strong, rules over the

Canadian Shield and summons the Aurora. He is likened to the Biblical King Nimrod, and the boreal forest groans at his approach. Hyperborea is said to be a fabulous northern land and, like Arcadia, a utopia where war and disease are unknown.[26] In the poet's mind, this could be a Canadian Arcadia.

It is not too great a stretch to say that Sangster thought Canada might be a special place where people could live closer to God. This national destiny was, perhaps, God's will, and God created Canada for this purpose. In this, our poet comes close to equating Canada to a New Jerusalem.[27] But his Christian faith never permits him to go that far.

Perhaps Sangster's most important achievement was to focus attention on Canada, its geography, its history, and its people. For him, the duty of the Canadian writer was to write about Canada. He chose to investigate all aspects—physical and metaphysical and spiritual—of the land beneath his feet. In his inaugural address at the Centre of Canadian Studies of the University of Edinburgh, presented on November 18, 1982, Malcolm Ross stated that "Ultimately, we are what we are because we are where we are. ... It was the first task for the Canadian imagination to possess the land ..."[28] Charles Sangster understood this. Catherine M. McLay, in her *Canadian Literature: the beginnings to the 20th century*, states: "As the literary heir of Goldsmith and Howe, and the predecessor of the Confederation poets, Charles Sangster established his reputation as 'Canada's national bard' ..."[29] As such, he occupied a crucial position, and his book had considerable influence on the poetry of those who came after. His "voyage of discovery" down the St. Lawrence and up the Saguenay helped inspire a generation of poets. The writers of the Confederation Period took up this task, as did the Group of Seven painters. In this way, they also "discovered" Canada—the real Canada.

Sangster, as noted, was born in 1822. Almost every Confederation Poet was born between 1857 and 1862, some four decades later. These younger poets, who established Canadian poetry on the foundations he laid, did not ultimately follow the older poet's lead. While several wrote extensively of the Canadian wilderness and the beauties of rural life—Isabella Valancy Crawford, Wilfred Campbell, Archibald Lampman, and Duncan Campbell Scott stand out—they turned west to English-speaking Ontario's portion of the Shield. In doing so they were facing the 20th century and the future while turning their backs on Canada's past.

What happened between the era of Sangster's vision, as set forth in *The St. Lawrence and the Saguenay, and Other Poems* in 1856, and the publication of Sir Charles G.D. Roberts' *Orion, and Other Poems* in 1880 was Confederation. The British North America Act of 1867 forever changed the future of Canada in ways our Fathers of Confederation could hardly have imagined. The "old" Canada of Québec and Ontario was replaced by a "new" Canada that would in four short years include British Columbia on the Pacific coast. As a result, the role played by French-Canadians, their culture and their history, was gradually reduced. And the Indigenous Peoples were left out of consideration. The chief culture of our future would be English-speaking, and the influence of the United States would grow.

There is considerable irony here. The chief point of Confederation was to keep the remaining British parts of North America free from the United States, a nation always looking to expand, and to keep Canada securely within the British Empire. Also, Canada was to be both Christian and conservative in order to avoid the revolutionary liberalism of her southern neighbour. Unfortunately, Confederation only delayed the process.

The Bay of Fundy and its Tantramar Marshes
The Beginning of a Canadian Literature

The Bay of Fundy and the sweeping Tantramar Marshlands that separate Nova Scotia from New Brunswick have played a seminal role in Canadian literature from the very beginning. Indeed, four important 19th century poets—Sir Charles G.D. Roberts, Bliss Carman, John Frederic Herbin, and Sophia M. Almon Hensley—wrote extensively about the beauty and history of this region and its people. In the case of Hensley, her finest nature poems are set on or near St. Marys Bay on the Nova Scotia side of Fundy, which she counted among her best-loved places. Also on the eastern side of Fundy we have the site of the poetry in Herbin's masterwork, *The Marshlands: Souvenir in Song of the Land of Evangeline*. Both Roberts and Carman set their major pieces on the great bay. In the case of Roberts it was his "Tantramar Revisited" and for Carman it was "Low Tide on Grand Pré."[1] These are two of the most-anthologized poems in Canadian literature, and deservedly so.

But before Roberts published "Tantramar Revisited" in *In Divers Tones* (1886) and Carman published "Low Tide on Grand Pré" in *Low Tide on Grand Pré: A Book of Lyrics* (1893), their cousin, Barry Bliss Straton, brought out his initial volume of poetry, *Lays of Love, and Miscellaneous Poems* (1884).[2] Like his two cousins, Straton attended Fredericton Collegiate School. Also like them, he loved the Bay of Fundy and its marshes. Unlike them, Straton chose farming over university. And he stayed in the area of his birth, believing that he had been fortunate to come from the finest place in Canada. So why leave?

Straton's poetry was accepted by William Douw Lighthall for his *Songs of the Great Dominion: Voices from the Forests and Waters, the Settlements and Cities of Canada* (1889),[3] and it was also included in Theodore H. Rand's *A Treasury of Canadian Verse* (1900).[4] A fine career lay before Straton, and he published two books of verse, but he died prematurely at age forty-seven on October 10, 1901 shortly after the publication of Rand's anthology, which established Straton's poetry internationally. Following his early death, his poetry continued to appear in important anthologies, such as *A Century of Canadian Sonnets*.[5] Nonetheless, Straton eventually faded from view, and today is a minor, largely unknown figure.

Although his poetry never attained the heights of the work of his fellow Confederation Poets, he is mentioned because he helped establish the marshlands of the Bay of Fundy in the literary imagination of the Canadian people, and he helped pave the way for poets like Roberts, Carman, Herbin, and Hensley.

Fundy and its marshes played a considerable role in the imaginations of many post-Confederation writers of the 20th century, especially those working in New Brunswick and Nova Scotia. Douglas Lochhead (1922–2011)[6] and John Thompson (1938–1976)[7] are two examples. And into the present century, the Fundy region continues to loom large in books by contemporary poets like Allan Cooper and Margaret Patricia Eaton. Canadian literature began here, in the Maritimes, when Sir Charles G.D. Roberts broke into print. Roberts' best poetry is set here, as is much of Carman's. Poets from this area have inspired a nation full of writers for over a hundred and forty years. And it all started with a farmer in York County, New Brunswick called Barry Straton. "Evening on the Marshes"[8] shows him at his best:

Evening on the Marshes

We have roamed the marshes, keen with expectation;
Lain at eve in ambush, where the ducks are wont to fly;
Felt the feverish fervor, the thrilling, full pulsation,
As the flocks came whirring from the rosy western sky.

All day long the sun with heat, and breeze with coolness,
Smote or kissed the grasses, and it seemed another lake
Flooded o'er the land and up the hills in fullness,
Shadows for the billows, sunshine for the waves that break.

Now beneath the pine, whose branches voice the breezes,
Passed the toil of day, we lie like gods in utter peace.
This is life's full nectar, this from care releases;
Oh, to rest for ever here where toil and tumult cease!

Slowly down the west the weary day is dying;
Slowly up the east ascends the mellow, mystic moon;
Swiftly swoop the hawks; the hooting owls are flying;
Through the darksome splendor breaks the lonesome cry
 of loon.

Ghost-like move the sails along the lake's long distance;
Faintly wafts the sailors' weirdsome song the waters o'er;
Faint the wavelets' music, as with low insistence,
Break they softly singing on the drowsy sandy shore.

Wooing us in whispers, water, earth and heaven—
Mystic whispers wafted o'er the darksome, waving deep—
Win us to themselves, our old creative leaven,
And we, mingling with them, softly sink to dreamless sleep.

European interest in the Bay of Fundy goes back to Samuel de Champlain's visit in 1605 and the founding of Port-Royal in the Annapolis Basin. Then follows over four hundred years of history. It is this rich story of joy and tragedy, of life and death, of war and peace, all linked to Fundy's great natural beauty, that drives much of the literature of Canada's Maritime region. The images created by poets like Straton, Roberts, Carman, and others linger in our literature and in our national consciousness. While Barry Straton may be forgotten, the books by his cousins still inspire emerging poets in the 21st century.

Sir Charles G.D. Roberts
Poet of the Tantramar

Sir Charles G.D. Roberts, KCMG, is commonly, and not incorrectly, known as the Father of Canadian Literature. He earned this title when, in 1880, he published *Orion, and Other Poems.*[1] Inspired by Roberts' example, other major Confederation Poets soon published their initial collections: Isabella Valancy Crawford in 1884, Archibald Lampman and Wilfred Campbell in 1888, Bliss Carman and Duncan Campbell Scott in 1893, and E. Pauline Johnson in 1895. By the turn of the century, there was a uniquely Canadian literature.

Roberts was born on January 10, 1860 at Douglas, New Brunswick, a farming community not far from Fredericton. He grew up, however, in the Tantramar Marsh area around the Bay of Fundy, his family having moved to Westcock when he was but a babe-in-arms. Many of his finest poems—as well as the best works by his cousin Bliss Carman—are set in the Fundean marshlands. Although his writing was interrupted by the First World War, in which he served as a Major, Roberts had published a dozen poetry collections, nine novels, nineteen collections of short stories, three volumes of history, five collections of stories for children, and a couple of guide books by the time he died on November 26, 1943, while another World War raged. At the end of that war, he was generally considered to be the greatest Canadian writer. Because of the popularity of his many books, Roberts was honoured with a knighthood by King George V.

From the above it is clear that the bulk of Roberts' writing was prose fiction, but today he is almost exclusively known as a poet. Like many other writers of the time, Roberts was the son of a minister, the Reverend George Goodridge Roberts, Anglican rector of the hamlet of Westcock. The future poet was largely educated at home prior to his time at the Fredericton Collegiate School, which was followed by the University of New Brunswick (B.A. 1879, M.A. 1881). He shared many of his father's values: Christianity, a support of all things British, and twofold loyalty to Queen and country. (Or at least he shared them when young.) Like many people during the Confederation Period, he was both a Canadian nationalist and a supporter of the Crown, the two not being mutually exclusive in those days. Roberts stood for an independent Canada within the British Empire.

As it had been with his father, the Reverend Roberts, the strict social conventions, religious duty, and traditional family obligations of the Victorian era—a wife and four children, a professorship at King's College in Windsor, Nova Scotia, income-producing free-lance writing, etc.—ruled the life of the poet until 1897 when he abruptly left his wife and children and moved to New York City. Perhaps inspired by his cousin, Bliss Carman, Roberts adopted a Bohemian lifestyle, living as a man-about-town in the United States, France, Germany, and England. He lived abroad until 1925 when, as a distinguished man of letters and popular author, he returned to Canada. He was sixty-five years old and had another ten books to write and publish.

Back in Canada, Roberts served as President of the Canadian Authors Association, which had been founded by Stephen Leacock and others four years earlier in 1921. He enjoyed the life of a senior figure of the Canadian cultural establishment. And he used his stature to help promote other Canadian writers.

Despite his elite place in Canadian literature, Roberts never lost sight of the farmers and fishermen of his native Tantramar. The most important, and best-loved, of his poems are the sonnets he wrote during the late 19th century. These include "The Sower" and "The Potato Harvest" from *In Divers Tones*[2] and "The Salt Flats," "The Pea-Fields," "The Mowing," "The Winter Fields," "In an Old Barn," "The Flight of the Geese," and "The Herring Weir" from

Songs of the Common Day.[3] Indeed, Tantramar was never far from his mind.

Although these poems are commonly available to readers, it's worth quoting a couple of sonnets that display Roberts' respect for the good, honourable labour of farming and fishing.

The Sower

A brown sad-coloured hillside, where the soil,
  Fresh from the frequent harrow, deep and fine,
  Lies bare; no break in the remote sky-line,
Save where a flock of pigeons streams aloft,
Startled from feed in some low-lying croft,
  Or far-off spires with yellow of sunset shine;
  And here the Sower, unwittingly divine,
Exerts the silent forethought of his toil.

Alone he treads the glebe, his measured stride
  Dumb in the yielding soil; and tho' small joy
    Dwell in his heavy face, as spreads the blind
Pale grain from his dispensing palm aside,
  This plodding churl grows great in his employ;—
    Godlike, he makes provision for mankind.

The Herring Weir

Back to the green deeps of the outer bay
  The red and amber currents glide and cringe,
  Diminishing behind a luminous fringe
Of cream-white surf and wandering wraiths of spray.
Stealthily, in the old reluctant way,
  The red flats are uncovered, mile on mile,
  To glitter in the sun a golden while.

Far down the flats, a phantom sharply gray,
The herring weir emerges, quick with spoil.
    Slowly the tide forsakes it. Then draws near,
    Descending from the farm-house on the height,
A cart, with gaping tubs. The oxen toil
    Sombrely o'er the level to the weir,
    And drag a long black trail across the light.

While many readers have noted how his Bay of Fundy sonnets remind them of the early sonnets of Wordsworth, the poems of Roberts are more earthy, more working class, and distinctly Canadian in subject and tone.[4] Roberts continued publishing poetry until two years before his death—his final book was *Canada Speaks of Britain and Other Poems of the War*[5]—and throughout his long career his spiritual home remained the Tantramar, and he carried the marshes with him in his childhood memories during all his years in New York, Paris, Munich, and London.

The above observations do not mean that Roberts could not write on other topics. Along with fellow Confederation poet Major Frederick George Scott, Roberts had a close-up view of trench warfare during the First World War[6] and he did write vividly about his life in New York City,[7] a considerably harsher place than his native New Brunswick. In New York, Roberts was a sort of urban vagabond, at least until he established himself in the American literary scene. But it is neither his American urban poetry nor his war poetry, although both present much very fine writing, that are of interest here, because, in a real sense, he was always the boy from the Tantramar.[8]

When the poet left for New York in 1897 there was, in Canada, a rather common notion as to what kind of country our newly-minted nation should be. As we see with our Confederation Poets in general, English-speaking Canada was to be Christian, British, often rural/agrarian, and independent within a united Empire (later the Commonwealth). Canadians would place civic duty before individualistic adventure. When he returned twenty-eight years later, Roberts found post-First World War Canada changed, and not in ways he accepted. The war experience also changed Roberts, again in ways he did not welcome. The world of the Victorians and the Edwardians was over.

For Roberts, Christianity had also suffered a change. His cousin Bliss Carman had followed his own distant cousin, Ralph Waldo Emerson, into a form of Transcendentalism. The cousins were especially close. (Both Carman and Roberts attended the Fredericton Collegiate School, where both studied under, and were influenced by, Sir George Robert Parkin, and both later graduated from the University of New Brunswick.) It is known that both poets read Emerson's essays, as did many writers at the time, and some of Emerson's ideas do enter Roberts' poetry, but not to the extent they do in the work of Carman. Although they were close, and they did influence each other, especially when they were younger,[9] the poetry of Roberts differs from the poetry of Carman in that Roberts' verse is more focused and matter-of-fact while Carman tends to be rather misty-eyed and dreamy. Roberts is the realist in the family; Carman is the romantic.

Because Roberts lived into his eighties, he outlived his vision of Canada. In the 1880s and 1890s when he began publishing his major works, his new nation was a largely rural amalgam of British North America and New France. When Roberts returned following the First World War, industrialization, urbanization, and immigration from other parts of Europe had begun to create modern Canada, a process that would only accelerate following the Second World War.

By the end of the Victorian period, Roberts had developed an idiosyncratic form of nature mysticism—his own "religion"—perhaps somewhat inspired by Emerson's seminal essay *Nature*.[10] Roberts came to believe that by contemplating the natural world he would receive direct revelations from Nature's God—or, if not a proper God, then from a primal or elemental force—and that he could interpret these to get at some overarching moral truth: a truth inherent in the physical universe. Through this process, the poet could become infused with the spirit of Nature.

For example, consider his poem "The Unsleeping" from his 1896 collection *The Book of the Native*:[11]

The Unsleeping

I soothe to unimagined sleep
The sunless bases of the deep.
And then I stir the aching tide
That gropes in its reluctant side.

I heave aloft the smoking hill;
To silent peace its throes I still.
But ever at its heart of fire
I lurk, an unassuaged desire.

I wrap me in the sightless germ
An instant or an endless term;
And still its atoms are my care,
Dispersed in ashes or in air.

I hush the comets one by one
To sleep for ages in the sun;
The sun resumes before my face
His circuit of the shores of space.

The mount, the star, the germ, the deep,
They all shall wake, they all shall sleep.
Time, like a flurry of wild rain,
Shall drift across the darkened pane.

Space, in the dim predestined hour,
Shall crumble like a ruined tower.
I only, with unfaltering eye,
Shall watch the dreams of God go by.

During the first five stanzas the poet considers all of Creation. By the end of the poem he overlooks God himself and is privy to Divine dreams.

In another poem from the same collection—"Earth's Complines" —the poet wanders Christ-like through a garden of white lilies while gaining spiritual wisdom. In the poem's final stanza he states:

> And a spell came out of space
> From the light of its starry place,
>   And I saw in the deep of my heart
> The image of God's face.

Hardly orthodox Christianity. Having liberated himself from the faith of his father, Roberts was free to leave his wife and children and go to the United States.

Although he published a great many books, the chief contribution made by Sir Charles G.D. Roberts was his celebration of the natural beauty of the Tantramar Marshlands of the Bay of Fundy and his affection for the people who lived and worked there. As the Father of Canadian Literature, he helped establish a view of what Canada could become. He served his country well.

Isabella Valancy Crawford

Poet of a Nation's Thanks

It is always difficult for readers in the 21st century to picture Canada during the Confederation era. Today the village of Paisley, Ontario, offers its residents Back Eddie's, a fair trade organic coffee roastery and organic and local food emporium, a Paisley Blues Festival that has featured musicians like Michael Pickett and Erin McCallum, and a museum in which artifacts of past generations are immaculately displayed. Clearly, much has changed over the past one hundred and sixty-five years. Things were rather different in 1857 when Dr. Stephen Crawford arrived from Ireland. Paisley had existed for a scant half-dozen years and was still a small scattering of log structures, scarcely more than raw shanties, at the confluence of the Saugeen and Teeswater Rivers. A decade prior to Confederation it was, in fact, the Canadian frontier. A year after Dr. Crawford established his medical practice in Paisley, his wife and family, including daughter Isabella, joined him in roughing it in the backwoods of what was then Canada West.[1] This was quite a change from the genteel Donnybrook neighbourhood of Dublin, where Isabella had been born on Christmas Day of 1850.

Although one could hardly expect Mrs. Crawford to enjoy the lack of amenities this new life offered, for the seven-year-old Isabella, the frontier was a realm of fascinating possibilities. The local Indigenous People almost made a pet of her and often brought her presents when they came into the village to consult the doctor. The future poet developed a life-long interest in the legends and stories of these first Canadians. "The Camp of Souls" is an example of her understanding of the Manitou myth of the original peoples of the Great Lakes region, and of their theology concerning life, love, death, and the mystery of the spirit. Another example of how her early memories informed her later poetry is "Said the Canoe," in which a canoe speaks of its Native makers. Finally, in "The Dark Stag," one of Crawford's finest poems, she tells of Native hunters bringing down a mighty stag, a most unusual topic for a Victorian woman. Crawford treats both hunter and prey with great dignity. It is impossible to think of these pieces being written had the poet not spent three or four of her formative years in Paisley. (All three of these poems were selected by Margaret Atwood for *The New Oxford Book of Canadian Verse in English.*[2]) Crawford returns again to the Manitou myth with a markedly erotic twist,[3] remarkable for an unmarried woman, or any woman, writing in 1884. "The Lily Bed"[4] presents a Native brave in a canoe approaching a bed of water lilies.

The Lily Bed

His cedar paddle, scented, red,
He thrust down through the lily bed;

Cloaked in a golden pause he lay,
Locked in the arms of the placid bay.

Trembled alone his bark canoe
As shocks of bursting lilies flew

Thro' the still crystal of the tide,
And smote the frail boat's birchen side;

Or, when beside the sedges thin
Rose the sharp silver of a fin;

Or when, a wizard swift and cold,
A dragon-fly beat out in gold

And jewels all the widening rings
Of waters singing to his wings;

Or, like a winged and burning soul,
Dropped from the gloom an oriole

On the cool wave, as to the balm
Of the Great Spirit's open palm

The freed soul flies. And silence clung
To the still hours, as tendrils hung,

In darkness carven, from the trees,
Sedge-buried to their burly knees.

Stillness sat in his lodge of leaves;
Clung golden shadows to its eaves,

And on its cone-spiced floor, like maize,
Red-ripe, fell sheaves of knotted rays.

The wood, a proud and crested brave;
Bead-bright, a maiden, stood the wave.

And he had spoke his soul of love
With voice of eagle and of dove.

Of loud, strong pines his tongue was made;
His lips, soft blossoms in the shade,

That kissed her silver lips—her's cool
As lilies on his inmost pool—

Till now he stood, in triumph's rest,
His image painted in her breast.

One isle, 'tween blue and blue did melt,—
A bead of wampum from the belt

Of Manitou—a purple rise
On the far shore heaved to the skies.

His cedar paddle, scented, red,
He drew up from the lily bed;

All lily-locked, all lily-locked,
His light bark in the blossoms rocked.

Their cool lips round the sharp prow sang,
Their soft clasp to the frail sides sprang,

With breast and lip they wove a bar.
Stole from her lodge the Evening Star;

With golden hand she grasped the mane
Of a red cloud on her azure plain.

It by the peaked, red sunset flew;
Cool winds from its bright nostrils blew.

They swayed the high, dark trees, and low
Swept the locked lilies to and fro.

With cedar paddle, scented, red,
He pushed out from the lily bed.

This poem is her sensuous *tour de force*.[5] Pieces like this, as well as other major Crawford poems, were sparked by her memories of life in Paisley, for Crawford, like other writers, kept her childhood near.

Around the age of puberty, Crawford moved with her family to Lakefield, a village in the Kawartha Lakes area north of Peterborough and the future home of Margaret Laurence, another Canadian woman to deal frankly with erotic subjects. It is here, on the banks of the Otonabee River, that the teenaged Crawford wrote her first poems, fairy tales,[6] and stories.[7] Although a mere village, two fine female writers lived in the immediate area: Susanna Moodie (1803–1885), who lived there during the 1830s, and Catharine Parr Traill (1802–1899), who would survive Crawford to die in Lakefield. In the case of Moodie, she published her initial poetry in 1830 and her first novel in 1853. Traill had begun publishing much earlier in 1818. The successful example of such strong women gave the young Crawford a boost. Perhaps she could also become a great writer of poetry and fiction, and publish books like they did. It was during these Lakefield years that the Dominion of Canada came into being via the British North America Act, an event that was of interest to the Crawford family and would lead to Crawford's poem "Canada to England" in which the poet celebrates the "strong bond between/ Two mighty lands" where "The bonds between us are no subtle links/ Of subtle minds" but "God's own seal of kindred ..."[8] Crawford's conservatism and her embracing of the imperial bond with England were common, and important, sentiments in the Confederation Period.

While Crawford could not have met Susanna Moodie, as the Moodies had left Lakefield prior to the arrival of the Crawford family, it is certain that she did know Catharine Parr Traill, as recorded in the Traill correspondence. Sadly, the exact extent of their relationship remains a mystery, and Dr. Crawford relocated to Peterborough in 1869. Crawford, although writing at the time, was just shy of her nineteenth birthday. Whatever the degree of interaction between the older writer and the budding poet, Crawford did value, and learn from, Traill's *The Backwoods of Canada*.[9] Perhaps more than any other volume of prose, Crawford used *Backwoods* for both information and inspiration.[10]

In all her poems, especially the pieces that directly connect to her years in Paisley and Lakefield, her nature imagery is vivid and precise. Although only a child, Crawford was a keen observer of the trees, lakes, rivers, and animals of both the Great Lakes region and the Kawartha Lakes, especially in the early years of Confederation when urban centres were distant and the backwoods near. While she was a Romantic and, of course, a Victorian, she developed a remarkable understanding of the daily life of the Indigenous People, of their camps, and of hunting and fishing.

Peterborough brought her some good fortune in terms of her writing, and by 1873 she tasted her first success, publishing "The Inspiration of Song" in *The Favorite*[11] and "The Vesper Star" in *The Mail*.[12] "The Inspiration of Song" is a poem set in eight stanzas, each stanza composed of eight decasyllabic lines, displaying the high Romanticism of its twenty-two-year-old author. It also reveals a young woman confident with language and well educated, possessed of a fine vocabulary and a knowledge of romantic fantasy and traditional poetic structures. "The Vesper Star," a blank-verse erotic allegory of twenty-two lines divided into two unequal stanzas, appeared on the eve on her twenty-third birthday. Although far from her finest work, this short piece offers some beautifully turned images. The sun just set behind the "round-browed mountain," we are presented with a mountain "Crowned with the snows of hawthorn, avalanched/ All down its sloping shoulder with the bloom/ Of orchards ..." In a typical romantic flourish, her twilight meditation closes with the brooding image "Of shadow, shadow, stretching everywhere."

Despite Peterborough being a town, rather than a simple village, Crawford was lonely. Her family was impoverished, no doubt the result of Dr. Crawford's immoderate drinking. Both Mrs. Crawford and her daughter were uncomfortable with company due to their narrow means and their shabby home and attire. Despite the explicit sexual imagery in her verse, there is no indication that Crawford ever had a lover, or even a casual boyfriend. Her family seemed to have been isolated from society. After the doctor died of a heart attack in July of 1875, there was little to keep what was left of his family in Peterborough.

By the summer of 1876, because of their increasing poverty, both mother and daughter had begun their tedious and depressing sequence of dismal Toronto boarding and rooming houses, moving often. The poet would die of heart failure in one of these on John Street on February 12, 1887, less than two months after her thirty-sixth birthday. The hard streets of Toronto were a long way from her idyllic childhood in pastoral Paisley or her teenage years in Lakefield. It was during her decade in Toronto that our poet, like Archibald Lampman, became concerned with the conflict between the teachings of Christianity and the emerging materialistic group of middle-class merchants and small industrialists for whom financial gain was primary. One example of this conflict in her poetry is "Wealth."[13]

Wealth

Wealth, doff thy jewelled crown of gold,
  Thy sceptre strong, nor rave;
I tell thee, Wealth, on Christian mould
  Thou canst not buy a slave.
Nay, tyrant, seek some other sod
For slaves to tremble at thy nod!

Hence, despot, with thy clanking chains!
  Thou canst not purchase here.
Seek brutal hinds on savage plains;
  We hold our poor men dear.
They shall not bend beneath thy yoke,
Nor cringe before thy sceptre's stroke.

God spake—we listened—loud His voice,
  High o'er the noise of waves.
Arose our answer: "Laud, rejoice,
  No more shall blood of slaves
Enrich our soil!" From sea to sea
Rolled God's grand watchword, "Liberty."

What! tyrant, dost thou linger yet
With sceptre and with crown?
Can it be thy mighty foot is set
On necks of men bowed down?
And dost thou smile with fierce lips locked?
Is God by despot Wealth still mocked?

Look down, O God! whence comes this train
Yoked to the tyrant's wheel?
Hark! dost Thou hear that clanking chain?
See yon gaunt wretches reel?
Art Thou not mocked, eternal God?
Are these not serfs on freedom's sod?

Out, fool! this is a Christian land,
And they but idly rave
Who clamour that yon grisly band
Contains a single slave;
Not one was bought in any mart,
None captive to the sword or dart.

Wealth is no despot, owns no slave;
No wretch must take his dole—
He hath a choice, the yawning grave—
Then answer, foolish soul,
Is Wealth a tyrant if he thrives
When famine strikes at lowly lives?

"Wealth" displays the poet's Red Tory, or perhaps more properly, her Tory social-democratic and Christian streak. One could, actually, view her as a Christian socialist, objecting in a most forceful manner to the reality of "wage-slavery"[14] and a developing underclass in the new nation. This variety of conservative socialism was not uncommon in the Canada of Crawford's era. What was uncommon, however, was for a woman to speak so frankly on socio-economic and political issues.

In spite of the failure of her self-financed book, probably due to poor editing and amateur marketing, Crawford had successfully placed her verse in *The Mail*, *The Evening Telegram*, *The National*, and *The Globe*, as well as American tabloids, which were widely read in those days. Although there was no money in poetry, she had established a public readership, especially in Toronto and wherever Toronto newspapers were sold. Unfortunately, Crawford did not live to see her work properly appreciated. In 1905 *The Collected Poems of Isabella Valancy Crawford* would be published to lasting acclaim. Of her decade in Toronto there is little record. Apparently, mother and daughter had almost completely withdrawn from society, and there is no indication that Crawford had significant contact with members of the Toronto literary community. Clearly, her time was spent almost totally on reading and writing.

Perhaps because of mother and daughter being so withdrawn, hardly any photographs exist of Crawford during her Toronto years, a period when she produced most of her best poetry and fiction. What pictures that do exist show a severe, somewhat plain, woman with rather short, dark hair. She is remembered by Seranus (the *nom de plume* of Susan Frances Harrison), the literary editor of *The Week*, as being "A tall, dark young woman, one whom most people would feel difficult, almost repellent in her manner."[15] But whatever disillusionment Crawford may have harboured because of a lack of financial reward, it was not manifest in her poetry. She would sing brightly to the end of her days.

In addition to the fact that Crawford left us several brilliant and beautiful poems, she also allows us to see the nature of Canadian ideas in the time of Confederation. That she was a Canadian patriot is clear from "The Rose of a Nation's Thanks."[16] This poem was written upon the return of troops from service during the Northwest Rebellion. Here the poet states "There is not a lad that treads in the gallant ranks/ Who does not already bear on his breast the Rose of a Nation's Thanks!" That she was committed to the British Crown *as well as* to a united Canada is clear from "Canada to England."[17] An Anglo-Irish family, the Crawfords were active in the tiny Christ Church in Lakefield. When the congregation outgrew its modest building, Dr. Crawford served on the committee to build a new church, St. John the Baptist. Following their removal to Peterborough, the Crawfords attended services in St. John's Anglican Church. Evidence of her religious feeling is clear throughout her poetry.

It is an error to think that the drive for Confederation was anti-British. The goal in the 19th century was to bring our nation together as British North America (*i.e.*, Canada), not to seek complete political independence, as the United States had done. Loyalty to both her new nation of Canada and the old nation across the Atlantic, loyalty to her Queen, a strong Anglican faith, and an opposition to the bitter oppression created by unjust accumulations of wealth, mark not just Crawford; these sentiments were the common currency of what was to be Canada in the years leading up to 1867. By reading and *enjoying* her poetry (for at its best it is enjoyable) we can appreciate the philosophical and spiritual elements that led to a united Canada, our version of North America.

Frederick George Scott

Poet of the Laurentians

Frederick George Scott was born in Montréal on April 7, 1861, served in and wrote about the First World War, and died in Québec City towards the end of the Second World War on January 19, 1944. During his life, Scott established himself as the leading English-language poet working in Québec, publishing a dozen volumes in Canada and Britain. Because of his vivid nature poems, he was called the Poet of the Laurentians. Despite his importance to Canadian letters there has been very little criticism, and the trend has been to dismiss, or categorize, Scott as a "Victorian" (as if that were a bad thing). Of course, people born in 1861 and raised during the 1860s and 1870s were Victorians by both birth and rearing, for the Queen held the throne until her death in 1901. His final book, a selection of his work called *Poems Old and New,*[1] was published in 1936. Even its most recent poems reflect the Victorian era in style and form despite the fact that these pieces were written at the close of the reign of King George V.

Although city-born, Scott was, as most boys are, interested in playing in parks, woodlots, and along riverbanks. In his case this interest in the natural world would last a lifetime. While his books have long gathered dust on forgotten shelves, his poem "The Unnamed Lake"[2] is never out-of-print. Indeed, of the ten poems selected by Wilfred Campbell for *The Oxford Book of Canadian Verse* (1913 edition), "The Unnamed Lake" was the sole poem to survive when Margaret Atwood re-edited *The New Oxford Book of Canadian Verse in English* in 1982. This is unfortunate because poems such as "The King's Bastion"[3] also deserve to be read. I present it here:

The King's Bastion

Quebec

Fierce on this bastion beats the noonday sun;
The city sleeps beneath me, old and grey;
On convent roofs the quivering sunbeams play,
And batteries guarded by dismantled gun.
No breeze comes from the Northern hills which run
Circling the blue mist of the Summer's day;
No ripple stirs the great stream on its way
To those dim headlands where its rest is won.

Ah God, what thunders shook these crags of yore,
What smoke of battle rolled about this place,
What strife of worlds in pregnant agony:
Now all is hushed, yet here, in dreams, once more
We catch the echoes, ringing back from space,
Of God's strokes forging human history.

Aside from the fact that this is a well-written piece, it also displays the poet's central themes. As has been much noted by scholars, the poetry of the Confederation Period is hallmarked by Canadian nationalism, Christian idealism, and nature imagery. Scott fits right in. After taking his B.A. (1881) and M.A. (1884) at Bishop's College, he read theology at King's College (London). A devoted Anglo-Catholic, he was eventually elevated to the position of Reverend Canon of St. Matthew's (Québec City). Although over fifty years of age, Scott joined the Army in 1914 and served as Chaplain of the Canadian 1st Division in the War to End All Wars. He held the rank of Major and in 1918 was awarded the D.S.O. for valour. As one might expect from an Anglican priest, God is never far from Scott's thoughts. He often discovered in the beauty and grandeur of nature a proof of God's goodness, and of God's active role in our world. In addition to his religious faith, he was both a Canadian patriot and a staunch supporter of the British Empire (now Commonwealth). As did most writers of his time—and many of the Fathers of Confederation, too—Scott believed both the Church of England and the Empire to be forces for good in human affairs.

Following the horrors of World War I and life at the Front,[4] Scott came to both celebrate the courage of his fellow soldiers and to lament the brutality of war. He would "weep as only strong men weep" at the sight of our glorious dead.[5] In this way, he was like Helena Coleman, who was one year his senior. Both wrote of the Great War and of its effect on Canada. Several other Confederation Poets published books both prior to and following this war; one thinks of Sir Charles G.D. Roberts, Bliss Carman, and Duncan Campbell Scott. This conflict left a deep mark on an entire generation of Canadians, both on the men who fought and the rest of society.

No family was untouched by the tragic events of 1914–1918. Few writers have explored the grief and loss of war more clearly than Frederick George Scott, whose son Henry Hutton Scott was killed during the Battle of the Somme. A fine example of Scott's poems showing the impact of the war would be his sonnet "Call Back Our Dead."[6]

Call Back Our Dead

Call back our Dead—the fateful feud is o'er;
   Call back our Dead, we need them here to-day,
   We need them in their freshness and their play,
Their valiant manhood ripened by the war.
Our hearts stand open; open, too, the door
   Of that still chamber where the shadow lay
   Since death's grim message came. No other ray
But their bright presence can the light restore.

Call back our Dead, they die each day we live—
Deep in our hearts they die the whole day long.
Call back our Dead, the welcoming hearth is bright,
All that this life can give them, we will give.
Tell them God's angels sing again their song
And Peace hangs out her star upon the night.

November 11th, 1925

Despite such cruelty and devastation, for Scott nature restores the soul, as his "In the Woods"[7] shows.

In the Woods

This is God's house—the blue sky is the ceiling,
This wood the soft green carpet for His feet,
Those hills His stairs, down which the brooks come stealing
With baby laughter, making earth more sweet.

And here His friends come, clouds and soft winds sighing,
And little birds whose throats pour forth their love,
And spring and summer, and the white snow lying
Pencilled with shadows of bare boughs above.

And here come sunbeams through the green leaves straying,
And shadows from the storm-clouds over-drawn,
And warm, hushed nights, when mother earth is praying
So late that her moon-candle burns till dawn.

Sweet house of God, sweet earth so full of pleasure,
I enter at thy gates in storm or calm;
And every sunbeam is a joy or treasure,
And every cloud a solace and a balm.

In Scott's view there is an obvious split between the world of nature and the world of human activity. While the poet can secure spiritual peace walking in the Laurentians, near which he lived, he contrasts this with the action of evil visible in human failings. This can lead to poetic pessimism, which was not unknown during the Victorian and Edwardian eras. But it can also lead to a deeper religious faith. At some point, most people, and certainly most poets, come to a spiritual crisis.

Well-known during his lifetime for his war poetry and for his hymns of national pride, today it is his nature poetry that speaks the loudest:

> It sleeps among the thousand hills
>   Where no man ever trod,
> And only nature's music fills
>   The silences of God.
>
> Great mountains tower above its shore,
>   Green rushes fringe its brim,
> And o'er its breast for evermore
>   The wanton breezes skim.
>
> Dark clouds that intercept the sun
>   Go there in Spring to weep,
> And there, when Autumn days are done,
>   White mists lie down to sleep.
>
> —from "The Unnamed Lake"[8]

His books inspired a generation of Canadian poets, none more important than his son, F.R. (Frank) Scott. Frederick George Scott's *Collected Poems*[9] was published in 1934. I wish it were still in print.

George Frederick Cameron:
The Classic Poet

Among the most respected poets of the Confederation Period was George Frederick Cameron. When Oxford University Press issued its initial *Oxford Book of Canadian Verse*[1] in 1913, its editor, Wilfred Campbell, included five of Cameron's poems. But by the time Margaret Atwood brought out her updated *The New Oxford Book of Canadian Verse in English* in 1982, Cameron had completely vanished. Nor is Cameron included in the otherwise excellent two-volume *Canadian Poetry* edited by Jack David and Robert Lecker. And even Carole Gerson and Gwendolyn Davies left him out of their exhaustive study, *Canadian Poetry: From the Beginnings Through the First World War*, which had done so much to revive the poetry of the otherwise forgotten Susan Frances Harrison, Helena Coleman, and Sophia M. Almon Hensley.

Nonetheless, Douglas Lochhead has noted that Cameron won the poetry prize of Queen's University[2] in 1883. And Archibald Lampman praised Cameron in "Two Canadian Poets"[3] for his poetic truth and his rare spontaneity, and ranked him alongside Sir Charles G.D. Roberts. Clearly Lampman, Campbell, Lochhead, and the staff of Queen's University considered Cameron to be an important poet worthy of our attention.

The contemporary reader faces a great barrier when it comes to the poetry of George Frederick Cameron. Our poet was born in New Glasgow, Nova Scotia on September 24, 1854. He died in Ontario of heart disease a week before his thirty-first birthday on September 17, 1885. Between his birth and early death, Cameron studied law in Boston and practised law in that city for five years, returned to Canada, studied at Queen's University, and served as editor of the

Daily News in Kingston. He also wrote the poems that would attract the praise of Archibald Lampman and form the contents of his posthumous collection. It was a busy few years. But because he died at age thirty, Cameron did not have time to prepare a book-length manuscript. His single volume of poetry, *Lyrics on Freedom, Love and Death*,[4] was produced posthumously by his brother and issued in Kingston in 1887 through the good offices of the *Daily News* newspaper. It is long out-of-print. As a result, readers of hardcopy are left with the five poems included in the 1913 edition of *The Oxford Book of Canadian Verse*.

Lyrics on Freedom, Love and Death, is extremely broad in its scope. It contains poems on Cuba, Russia, France, Colombia, and Ireland. Other poems deal with love; other writers (Edgar Allan Poe, John Milton, Lord Byron, Shelley); friends and family; death; sacred matters and human fate. Over 160 poems are included. Many of these pieces show the influence of Tennyson, the current Poet Laureate.

Cameron, although a young man, asked searching spiritual questions. A few poem titles illustrate this: "Is There a God?," "My Faith," "Lord God Almighty," "He Is Risen," "To God the Auditor of All Accounts," and "My Fate." This last poem, "My Fate," was actually the poet's death poem, found in his pocket.[5] It shows the power of his verse:

My Fate

Away and beyond that point of pines,
    Away in a spot where the glad grapes be,
Purple and pendant on verdant vines,
    That Fate of mine is awaiting me.

And if no more the wind blows true
    To waft me afar to that island sweet,
Beyond that greater and other blue
    I feel that I and my fate shall meet.

For the hope that is can never fade,
And the hope that is can never fall,
That Fate was law since the world was made,
That it shall be law till the end of all.

And Time may be long or it may be brief
Ere I stand on that dim and unknown shore,
And grief or joy be mine, but grief
Can dwell not there—where we meet once more.

"My Fate" does not, however, answer the question of Cameron's relationship to Christian theology. "My Faith" is an earlier poem that may throw some light on his religious ideas:[6]

My Faith

I would not blot the star of Hope
That hangs so palely in the skies:
But, giving thought a larger scope,
And following wheresoe'er it flies,

I find I hate nor sects nor creeds,
Yet have a creed all creeds above,
Whose faith consists in noble deeds,
Whose highest law is highest love.

And thus I do not feign, but feel
A different faith from thee, my friend!
And yet, perhaps, through woe and weal
They both lead on to one grand end.

"My Faith," in which the "highest law is highest love," echoes another Cameron poem, "Standing on Tiptoe," in which the poet states:[7]

I hold at length the only future—Truth,
  And Truth is Love.

These ideas call to mind both the Biblical affirmation that "God is love" and the Keatsian observation, central to Romanticism since the 1820 publication of his "Ode on a Grecian Urn," that "Beauty is truth, truth beauty."[8]

Indeed, the three words *love, truth,* and *beauty* are crucial to Cameron's poetic vision. He always had one foot in the realm of Romanticism and the other foot in the world of Christian and classical thought.[9] In this way he was like many others among his fellow Confederation Poets. Most enjoyed the benefit of a classical university education (in Cameron's case, Boston University's School of Law and later, upon his return to Canada, Queen's University) and most cut their creative teeth on the great 19th century Romantics: Wordsworth, Keats, Byron, and Shelley. This led them to a problem characteristic of their age: the spirituality of the Christian and classical world leads to God; the spiritual quest in Romanticism leads to man. Usually, when a writer recognizes such a duality of thought, it serves as an impetus to seek a resolution. Because Cameron died so young, he never worked very far towards any reintegration of his two divergent paths.

Other poets faced the same conundrum. Archibald Lampman struggled to relate, or integrate, his Anglicanism and his Romanticism, in his case German as well as English Romanticism. The same was true for Sir Charles G.D. Roberts, who eventually abandoned his Anglicanism completely. What Cameron does not share with any of his contemporaries is that he has no nature poetry or poems touching on the Canadian landscape. This makes him unique. His poetry is almost entirely either a literature of ideas and introspection (from his Christian and classic background) or a literature of emotions and feelings (from his 19th century Romantic leanings). Up until Modernism became firmly established in Canada following the devastation and trauma of the First World War, the poetry of George Frederick Cameron was regularly included in anthologies, both for the general reader and for use in our high schools and universities. It still deserves inclusion.

William Douw Lighthall

Poet of the Songs

William Douw Lighthall was born in Hamilton, Canada West (as Ontario was known then) on December 27, 1857. His family moved to Montréal, where he studied law at McGill University (B.A. in 1879, M.A. in 1885). He then practised law in that city until 1944. Lighthall died in Montréal a decade later on August 3, 1954. A well-respected lawyer, he is, however, known to us for his vital contribution to Canadian literature. It was as a man of letters that he became a Fellow of the Royal Society of Canada in 1902. And he went on to serve as the president of that body, 1918–1919.

Although Lighthall was a published poet, and a genuine member of the Confederation generation, he will always be remembered for the ground-breaking anthology, *Songs of the Great Dominion: Voices from the Forests and Waters, the Settlements and Cities of Canada*,[1] which he edited in 1889. This collection was published in London (England), and it established the Confederation Poets as the voice of the newly minted Canada. It included such leading poets as: George Frederick Cameron, Wilfred Campbell, Bliss Carman, Isabella Valancy Crawford, Susan Frances Harrison (writing as Seranus), E. Pauline Johnson, Archibald Lampman, Sir Charles G.D. Roberts, Duncan Campbell Scott, and Frederick George Scott.[2] Several of the most important poems of the Confederation Period were included, such as Campbell's "Indian Summer" and "Vapour and Blue," Carman's "Low Tide on Grand Pré," Lampman's "Heat" and "The Frogs," and Roberts' "Tantramar Revisited." Indeed, *Songs of the Great Dominion* set the stage for the publication of both Wilfred Campbell's *The Oxford Book of Canadian Verse* in 1913 and John W. Garvin's *Canadian Poets*[3] in 1916 because it was Lighthall who identified the Confederation Poets as Canada's seminal group. Lighthall did his work so well that for over half a century, anthologists and scholars referred to *Songs of the Great Dominion* when they surveyed our poetry.

What set Lighthall apart from Campbell were his bold perceptiveness and his decision to never play it safe. He took risks. In 1889, the Confederation Poets were hardly known in Canada, and certainly unknown in England, where his anthology was to be published. Cameron's book had been published only two years before in 1887, Campbell's and Lampman's first collections only one year before in 1888, and Bliss Carman, Pauline Johnson, and Duncan Campbell Scott did not publish their initial books until the 1890s. Yet, almost every poet Lighthall included went on to become crucial in the establishment of a truly Canadian culture.

Perhaps the most insightful aspect of *Songs of the Great Dominion* is to be found in Lighthall's lengthy introduction.[4] He sees *four* groups as being central to the establishment of a genuine Canadian people: the Indigenous Peoples, the early French settlers, the original English settlers, and the 35,000 United Empire Loyalists who arrived following the American Revolution. These Loyalists came from diverse ethnic, religious, and cultural backgrounds. In Lighthall's view, these four groups put aside their differences, at least to some extent, to form a united nation, and to work towards Confederation. The act of Confederation in 1867 ushered in feelings of exultation and confidence; his time was a time of hopefulness.[5]

Foreshadowing The Group of Seven painters and scholars of Confederation poetry like Malcolm Ross, Lighthall understood that the nature of the land and its climate shaped the human culture of the settlers. Canada has a unique geography; it is not England, nor is it France. Nor can it be exactly like the United States. To live properly in our distinct geography was to *become* Canadian. In seeking a full understanding of North America, the Canadian People, as a distinct people, and the Canadian culture they would develop, were destined to take a different path than the one embarked upon by the revolutionary nation to the south.[6] This emphasis on the natural landscape of Canada and on nature poetry, so visible in the work of most Confederation Poets, continued into the Great Generation. Poets like Milton Acorn, who was inspired by Archibald Lampman, and Raymond Souster, who was inspired by both Lampman and Wilfred Campbell, became leading nature poets during the last half of the 20th century. And perhaps one can see that Bliss Carman's "In Apple Time"[7] was the spark that ignited Al Purdy's "Selling Apples."[8]

Songs of the Great Dominion was not the very first gathering of Canadian poetry. That honour belongs to the Reverend E.H. Dewart's *Selections from Canadian Poets*[9] in 1864, three years prior to Confederation. In addition to the fact that the Confederation Poets do not appear in Dewart's anthology, there is a new note of patriotism in *Songs of the Great Dominion* largely absent from the earlier book. This quality of national feeling, sparked by the act of Confederation (*i.e.*, the British North America Act), was noted by Carole Gerson and Gwendolyn Davies in their "Afterword" to *Canadian Poetry: From the Beginnings Through the First World War*[10] in which they comment on "the growing cultural nationalism of the post-Confederation era." Indeed, in Lighthall's volume they see a cheerful spirit of national consciousness in the young poets he discovered. And this predominance of nationalism and idealism continued into the early 20th century in the poetry collected in Campbell's *The Oxford Book of Canadian Verse*[11] in 1913.

Lighthall also shared these feelings of pride and excitement. His poem "The Confused Dawn"[12] is one example.

The Confused Dawn

(1882)

YOUNG MAN.

What are the Vision and the Cry
That haunt the new Canadian soul?
Dim grandeur spreads we know not why
O'er mountain, forest, tree and knoll,
And murmurs indistinctly fly.—
Some magic moment sure is nigh.
O Seer, the curtain roll!

SEER.

The Vision, mortal, it is this—
Dead mountain, forest, knoll and tree
Awaken all endued with bliss,
A native land—O think!—to be—
Thy native land—and ne'er amiss,
Its smile shall like a lover's kiss
From henceforth seem to thee.

The Cry thou couldst not understand,
Which runs through that new realm of light,
From Breton's to Vancouver's strand
O'er many a lovely landscape bright,
It is their waking utterance grand,
The great refrain "A NATIVE LAND!"—
Be thine the ear, the sight.

But unlike many of his fellow Confederation Poets, Lighthall included both the French and English components in his vision of the new nation. In "Montreal"[13] he unites the French reality (the saint and chevalier) with the English/British tradition (the Scarlet Tunic) into a common patriotism.

Montreal

Reign on, majestic Ville-Marie!
    Spread wide thine ample robes of state;
    The heralds cry that thou art great,
And proud are thy young sons of thee.
Mistress of half a continent,
    Thou risest from thy girlhood's rest;
    We see thee conscious heave thy breast
And feel thy rank and thy descent.

Sprung of the saint and chevalier!
    And with the Scarlet Tunic wed!
    Mount Royal's crown upon thy head;
And—past thy footstool—broad and clear
    St. Lawrence sweeping to the sea;
    Reign on, majestic Ville-Marie!

Lighthall was keen to promote the idea that Canadian writers should be encouraged to write about Canada for their fellow Canadians. That is one reason behind his *Songs of the Great Dominion*. He was, of course, aware of the glories of Europe and of European art and culture. But he preferred Canada as the following poem shows.

My Native Land

Rome, Florence, Venice—noble, fair and quaint,
    They reign in robes of magic round me here;
But fading, blotted, dim, a picture faint,
    With spell more silent, only pleads a tear.
Plead not! Thou hast my heart. O picture dim!
    I see the fields, I see the autumn hand

Of God upon the maples! Answer Him
    With weird, translucent glories, ye that stand
Like spirits in scarlet and in amethyst!
I see the sun break over you; the mist
    On hills that lift from iron bases grand
    Their heads superb!—the dream, it is my native land.[14]

A full collection of Lighthall's own poetry, *Old Measures: Collected Verse*,[15] appeared in 1922, and remains the standard text for his work. Through his own poetry, and through his editing, Lighthall did more to shape the Canadian canon than any other 19th century man of letters.

Archibald Lampman

Poet on the Cusp of Modernism

the one true English-Canadian classic poet
—Raymond Souster

Archibald Lampman was born at Morpeth, Canada West (now Ontario) on November 17, 1861. He died of heart failure at the young age of thirty-seven in Ottawa on February 10, 1899. Because most of the Confederation Poets lived into the era of Modernism, Lampman, along with Isabella Valancy Crawford and George Frederick Cameron, represent the Confederation view of Canada in its most pure form, having died in the 1800s. Or, to state it another way, their "True North" is uncorrupted by 20th century cultural, political, and religious developments, such as the advent of early Modernism.

Canada's national myth—The True North—or at least the term itself, is derived from Alfred, Lord Tennyson, as noted by Terry Barker in his brief essay, "Tracking the True North"[1] in *Canadian Stories.* Lampman, being inspired by such English Romantics as Wordsworth and Keats in addition to the later Victorians like Tennyson and Arnold, his actual contemporaries, would know The True North connects to both Tennyson's poetic vision and to Tennyson's version of the Arthurian legend.[2] In the late 19th century, there was a general unity concerning what The True North, and thus Canada, was and might become. This unity all changed with the 20th century and the social and spiritual trauma of the First World War. Thereafter, various True Norths were created. Indeed, Confederation Poets like Bliss Carman and Sir Charles G.D. Roberts helped develop these "new" True Norths.

To understand Canada and Canadian culture, it is essential to understand the work of poets like Lampman, Crawford, and Cameron. Crawford was interested in both Irish and British Romanticism, having been born in Dublin in 1850. Lampman was, as noted above, influenced by the great English Romantics, but while at university he also looked into the southern-German Romantics of the Swabian School, such as the Lutheran pastor and lyric poet Eduard Mörike (1804–1875).[3] (A popular collection of Mörike's poems, *Gedichte*, had been published in 1838.) This German connection added a different edge to Lampman's poetry. Importantly, in his mature work, our poet could combine the youthful enthusiasm of Romantics like Keats with the sober gravity of the later Victorians. He could enjoy the best of both worlds.

All of the Confederation Poets were influenced, to one degree or another, by the great English Romantics, like Wordsworth, Keats, and Shelley, as well as the major Victorian poets, like the Poet Laureate of their era, Alfred, Lord Tennyson, Matthew Arnold, and the two Brownings. Lampman and his colleagues, however, realized two things. First, these 19th century British poets were continuing the tradition of English literature. The Confederation Poets knew they were *creating* the foundation for a Canadian literature. Secondly, they knew Canada was very different from the British Isles, and that Canadian literature, while sharing a language, had to be rooted in a Canadian reality. A true Canadian poetry could not afford to be derivative.

The most obvious differences were landscape and climate. This explains why almost every Confederation Poet wrote a body of nature poetry. No one would mistake Lampman's Canadian Shield for the Lake District of Wordsworth. As our Confederation Poets matured they also noted social differences. Canada might be part of the British Empire, but it was not a little England. Because they were both touched by genius, and because they died prior to the 20th century, I consider Archibald Lampman and Isabella Valancy Crawford to be key to any understanding of Canada and our culture.

As early as 1889, William Douw Lighthall noted four groups as being key to the establishment of a genuine Canadian people, a people who would over time develop a culture distinct from the cultures of the French and English founding nations, and also different from the United States, namely: (1) Canada's Indigenous Peoples, who had lived here for thousands of years, (2) the French settlers, (3) the early English settlers, and, after the American Revolution, (4) the United Empire Loyalists.[4] These people would become Canadians, a new people for their new nation. It is obvious from their writings that Crawford and Lampman understood this. Since these poets were visionaries, they saw that Canada would have a different destiny than that of the British Empire. While the term "The True North" came from Tennyson, its qualities would be discovered by Canadian writers. Their question was, therefore: What was Canada and what would Canada become?

In his discussion of Lampman's writings, L.R. Early observed that our poet had a deep affinity for the Romantics, a Keatsian belief in the spiritual unity of Truth and Beauty, and an insistence that poetry should express the character of the poet.[5] I would say that our poetry should also express the character of the Canadian people, not simply that of the individual poet. While this view is true of Lampman, it can also be said of most of our other writers of the Confederation Period. Although the Romantics might have been replaced by sterner Victorian sensibilities by the late 19th century, they still captivated the poetic imagination.

Even though Lampman wrote several insightful essays and lectures, a delight to read and often quoted by critics, the final test of any poet is the *poetry.* When Lampman wrote an essay or delivered a public lecture, he was mindful of his readers/listeners. He was speaking to them. But when he wrote a poem he was speaking to his heart. It is in poetry that Lampman reveals both himself and his deepest thoughts on Canada and its fledgling culture. When Lampman addressed Canada's landscape, he often appeared to prefer the austere Canadian Shield to the more pastoral cultivated land where he grew up in southern Ontario.[6] Of course, both were central to his vision of Canada.

Lampman was born on the shore of Lake Erie at Morpeth, where his father served as an Anglican minister. He later lived on the shore of Lake Ontario at Cobourg and, later still, Port Hope. His life on the southern fringe of Ontario left a lasting mark on his poetry. His initial literary adventures took place at Trinity College, University of Toronto, when he contributed to *Rouge et Noir.* Trinity is one of two Anglican colleges of the university. There the young man studied classics, not theology; he clearly had a literary career in mind. Nonetheless, Anglicanism also left its lasting impression on his thinking.

The Confederation Poets lived at an interesting time. As the 19th century deepened, change permeated the literary atmosphere. Our poets caught the end of the Romanticism of William Wordsworth (British Poet Laureate, 1843–1850), still very much in vogue when they commenced writing, and the blossoming of the sober Victorian era of Alfred, Lord Tennyson (Poet Laureate, 1850–1892). They also witnessed the attacks on Christian theology by rationalism. And they lived during the period of increased urbanization and industrialism in Canada. They saw the sons of farmers grow up to become factory labourers. Lampman was a man of contradictions. He was torn between the Anglican faith of his youth and scientific questioning. He was torn between the city (Ottawa), where he worked and lived, and the Canadian Shield, still largely a wilderness in the 1890s. Finally, in terms of poetry, Lampman had his heart firmly in the realm of Keats while his mind tended to drift toward a less passionate Tennysonian stance. And he was unsure how Canada should develop as his young country moved in the direction of enhanced national self-consciousness. On a more personal level, our poet was torn between his duty to his wife and the mother of their children, Maud, and to the woman to whom he addressed his most intense love lyrics, Katherine Waddell.[7]

At the time of his death in 1899, Lampman had started to develop a vision of what he hoped Canada would become, and a growing fear a different fate lay in wait. But his vision, even if it did not come to pass, was what many writers and artists believed during the late 19th century.

Lampman wrote a great deal of nature poetry. And here we come upon the first of his conflicts. Because he grew up in southern

Ontario, the landscapes of the north shore of Lake Erie, the north shore of Lake Ontario, and the Niagara Peninsula were dear to him. This was land long settled by English-Canadians and the United Empire Loyalists. Thus, it had already been greatly changed by human activity. A typical example of Lampman's nature poetry set where he grew up is "A Niagara Landscape."[8]

A Niagara Landscape

Heavy with haze that merges and melts free
  Into the measureless depth on either hand,
  The full day rests upon the luminous land
In one long noon of golden reverie.
Now hath the harvest come and gone with glee.
  The shaven fields stretch smooth and clean away,
  Purple and green, and yellow, and soft gray,
Chequered with orchards. Farther still I see
Towns and dim villages, whose roof-tops fill
  The distant mist, yet scarcely catch the view.
Thorold set sultry on its plateau'd hill,
    And far to westward, where yon pointed towers
  Rise faint and ruddy from the vaporous blue,
    Saint Catharines, city of the host of flowers.

Upon moving to Ottawa to work in the Post Office Department, with the encouragement of fellow poet Duncan Campbell Scott, Lampman discovered the Canadian Shield. Like Tom Thomson and the Group of Seven painters in the next century, and like Charles Sangster before him, our poet came to believe that this was, in some sense, the real Canada, or the real True North. It was Canada unspoiled by settlers from Britain and Europe. To this day, Lampman's poetry of the north is unexcelled. Such poems as "In the Wilds," "Temagami," "On Lake Temiscamingue," and "Night in the Wilderness" became standard anthology pieces. "Temagami"[9] is a fine example.

Temagami

Far in the grim Northwest beyond the lines
That turn the rivers eastward to the sea,
Set with a thousand islands, crowned with pines,
Lies the deep water, wild Temagami:
Wild for the hunter's roving, and the use
Of trappers in its dark and trackless vales,
Wild with the trampling of the giant moose,
And the weird magic of old Indian tales.
All day with steady paddles toward the west
Our heavy-laden long canoe we pressed:
All day we saw the thunder-travelled sky
Purpled with storm in many a trailing tress,
And saw at eve the broken sunset die
In crimson on the silent wilderness.

This was the land of the Indigenous Peoples, and you had to take it on its own terms. It was pure. It could be both "grim" and good. The final six lines of his sonnet, "In the Wilds,"[10] makes this obvious:

The savage vigour of the forest creeps
Into our veins, and laughs upon our lips;
The warm blood kindles from forgotten deeps,
And surges tingling to the finger tips.
The deep-pent life awakes and bursts its bands;
We feel the strength and goodness of our hands.

It is inevitable that readers find in Lampman two Canadas: the original land he discovered on Lake Temiscamingue and the "new" Canada created by the settlers. He needed both. His job was in Ottawa, as were his wife and children. And his literary career was based in Ottawa, Toronto, and Boston. On the other hand, he only felt liberated in the unbroken forests. It is there he came alive and was at one with God.

The son of an Anglican rector, Lampman developed his own nature-based appreciation of God. In this, Lampman's view is reminiscent of the teaching of Abbot Anthony, the hermit:[11]

> My book is the nature of created things,
> and any time I want to read the words of God,
> the book is before me.

Thus, Lampman was much like his older colleague at the Canadian post office, the pre-Confederation poet Charles Sangster, who made his spiritual discovery at Lac Saint-Jean, not Lake Temiscamingue.

Lampman's Christianity developed a mystical tone, as did his veneration of nature. The early influence of the Lutheran Eduard Mörike might have played a role here for Mörike also wrote of nature as in the pastoral landscape of southern Germany. Of course, William Wordsworth, a major influence on Lampman, was also quite the nature mystic. Lampman was able to combine German and British romanticisms in his finest poetry. At his job in Ottawa, Lampman seemed distant from God, removed from the spirit of the Divine that he increasingly found only in the natural world. Therefore, our poet took many canoe trips, sometimes with Duncan Campbell Scott, along the upper reaches of the Ottawa River and into Algonquin Park, the places that would give Tom Thomson his central idea of Canada. Lampman was never able to resolve the tension between the city and the forest.

Over time, Lampman came to see that the most likely future for Canada would not be a happy one. In "The City of the End of Things"[12] urbanization, and especially mass industrial production and the society shaped by such industry, eventually destroy civilization. All that is left of humanity by the end of the poem is "the grim Idiot at the gate ... deathless and eternal there." Even nature appears to be overcome. This is the ultimate dystopian poem.

The City of the End of Things

Beside the pounding cataracts
Of midnight streams unknown to us
'Tis builded in the leafless tracts
And valleys huge as Tartarus.
Lurid and lofty and vast it seems;
It hath no rounded name that rings,
But I have heard it called in dreams
The City of the End of Things.

Its roofs and iron towers have grown
None knoweth how high within the night,
But in its murky streets far down
A flaming terrible and bright
Shakes all the stalking shadows there,
Across the walls, across the floors,
And shifts upon the upper air
From out a thousand furnace doors;
And all the while an awful sound
Keeps roaring on continually,
And crashes in the ceaseless round
Of a gigantic harmony.
Through its grim depths re-echoing
And all its weary height of walls,
With measured roar and iron ring,
The inhuman music lifts and falls.
Where no thing rests and no man is,
And only fire and night hold sway;
The beat, the thunder and the hiss
Cease not, and change not, night nor day.
And moving at unheard commands,
The abysses and vast fires between,
Flit figures that with clanking hands

Obey a hideous routine;
They are not flesh, they are not bone,
They see not with the human eye,
And from their iron lips is blown
A dreadful and monotonous cry;
And whoso of our mortal race
Should find that city unaware,
Lean Death would smite him face to face,
And blanch him with its venomed air:
Or caught by the terrific spell,
Each thread of memory snapt and cut,
His soul would shrivel and its shell
Go rattling like an empty nut.

It was not always so, but once,
In days that no man thinks upon,
Fair voices echoed from its stones,
The light above it leaped and shone:
Once there were multitudes of men,
That built that city in their pride,
Until its might was made, and then
They withered age by age and died.
But now of that prodigious race,
Three only in an iron tower,
Set like carved idols face to face,
Remain the masters of its power;
And at the city gate a fourth,
Gigantic and with dreadful eyes,
Sits looking toward the lightless north,
Beyond the reach of memories;
Fast rooted to the lurid floor,
A bulk that never moves a jot,
In his pale body dwells no more,
Or mind, or soul,—an idiot!

But sometime in the end those three
Shall perish and their hands be still,
And with the master's touch shall flee
Their incommunicable skill.
A stillness absolute as death
Along the slacking wheels shall lie,
And, flagging at a single breath,
The fires that moulder out and die.
The roar shall vanish at its height,
And over that tremendous town
The silence of eternal night
Shall gather close and settle down.
All its grim grandeur, tower and hall,
Shall be abandoned utterly,
And into rust and dust shall fall
From century to century;
Nor ever living thing shall grow,
Nor trunk of tree, nor blade of grass;
No drop shall fall, no wind shall blow,
Nor sound of any foot shall pass:
Alone of its accursèd state,
One thing the hand of Time shall spare,
For the grim Idiot at the gate
Is deathless and eternal there.

Another unresolved area of conflict was between the Romanticism of Wordsworth and Keats on the one hand and the less passionate, and perhaps more realistic, Victorian literary outlook of Tennyson and Arnold on the other. Lampman truly wanted the Romantic view to be correct. But he suspected that it would not prove sustainable in the age of science, and he feared the Victorians were the future. They offered a culture of doubt, of uncertainty, of questioning traditional values, and of a materialism our poet found uncomfortable. Yet, in many of his non-nature poems he was drawn to the Victorians. As L.R. Early has written, "in general, Lampman learned much from the Romantics that he put to good use, and much from the Victorians that he put to bad."[13] Unfortunately for Lampman, Romanticism's day would soon be over.

As the 19th century drew to a close, traditional Christian theology was under attack. Many people attended church as unbelievers. They did so out of habit or for social reasons. Not immune from the spirit of the times, Lampman also questioned his Anglican traditions. And his attachment to Christian virtue suffered when he switched his affections from his wife, Maud, to Katherine Waddell, something he knew to be wrong, but could not resist.

The great value of Archibald Lampman is that he displays, at his best, an understanding of the vision of The True North that animated the men and women who drove Canada towards Confederation a century and a half ago. He also issues a warning about the emerging "new Canada" of the 20th century, a vision of Canada that would change The True North Tennyson had hailed in 1873. This is why just over a century after Tennyson wrote those words, Raymond Souster called Lampman "the one true English-Canadian classic poet we possess."[14] Lampman recalls the founding idea of Canada. More than any other poet, Lampman, like the artist Tom Thomson, could discern our land's spirit or soul. This was a spirit that animated this place thousands of years before European settlers arrived from France a mere four centuries ago. Lampman thought that any society created in the new nation should respect and be based, at least in part, on this primal spirit—The True North, if you will—and he thought Canadians should not simply adopt the errors of the British or the Americans. While our English-Canadian writers would share in the rich tradition of English-language literature, Lampman sought to influence Canada's new national self-consciousness in the direction of a culture uniquely Canadian. On the cusp of our modern world, his was a poetry of cautious hope.

Wilfred Campbell

Poet of the Lake Region

William Wilfred Campbell, the son of an Anglican priest, was thought to have been born in Berlin (now Kitchener) in Canada West (now Ontario) *circ.* 1858, although more recent research suggests he may have been born in Newmarket during 1860. The reports of his birth are unclear both in terms of location and date. Be that as it may, he certainly was related to the Duke of Argyll,[1] himself a poet of some note, who served as Governor General of Canada for five years (1878–1883) during Campbell's early manhood. This connection was a source of considerable pride for the young poet. Campbell graduated from secondary school in Owen Sound, a lovely town set at the foot of the Bruce Peninsula on Georgian Bay, in his day a remarkably beautiful and still wild or semi-wild district. That Campbell spent several of his formative years in what he called "the Canadian Lake Region"[2] is important because today he is respected as a poet of nature, and no other poet wrote as well about the Lake Huron-Bruce Peninsula-Georgian Bay area. His love of the Lake Region, and of the season of autumn, is clearly seen in "Lake Huron, October."[3]

Lake Huron, October

Miles and miles of lake and forest,
   Miles and miles of sky and mist,
Marsh and shoreland where the rushes
   Rustle, wind and water kissed;
Where the lake's great face is driving,
   Driving, drifting into mist.

Miles and miles of crimson glories,
  Autumn's wondrous fires ablaze;
Miles of shoreland red and golden,
  Drifting into dream and haze;
Dreaming where the woods and vapours
  Melt in myriad misty ways.

Miles and miles of lake and forest,
  Miles and miles of sky and mist;
Wild birds calling where the rushes
  Rustle, wind and water kissed;
Where the lake's great face is driving,
  Driving, drifting into mist.

This poem catches perfectly the feeling of being on the shore of either Lake Huron or Georgian Bay in late autumn with mist and chill in the air, the maples blazing, and no one else around. Indeed, although our population today is much greater, one can still experience this scene a century and a quarter later.

By far his most-anthologized poem is "Indian Summer."[4] It has never been out of print and inspires budding poets to the present day.

Indian Summer

Along the line of smoky hills
  The crimson forest stands,
And all the day the blue-jay calls
  Throughout the autumn lands.

Now by the brook the maple leans
  With all his glory spread,
And all the sumachs on the hills
  Have turned their green to red.

Now by great marshes wrapt in mist,
  Or past some river's mouth,
Throughout the long, still autumn day
  Wild birds are flying south.

While the above celebration of autumn is highly romantic and much in keeping with British nature poetry of the time, Campbell also recognized the harshness of nature. In "The Winter Lakes" a more strident note is sounded. The theme of brutal or stark nature is developed further in poems like "How One Winter Came in the Lake Region" in his next collection. Even a softer piece like his sonnet "Morning on the Shore"[5] ends in winter and death:

Morning on the Shore

The lake is blue with morning; and the sky
  Sweet, clear, and burnished as an orient pearl.
  High in its vastness scream and skim and whirl
White gull-flocks where the gleaming beaches die
Into dim distance, where great marshes lie.
  Far in ashore the woods are warm with dreams,
  The dew-wet road in ruddy sunlight gleams,
The sweet, cool earth, the clear blue heaven on high.

Across the morn a carolling school-boy goes,
Filling the world with youth to heaven's stair;
  Some chattering squirrel answers from his tree;
But down beyond the headland, where ice-floes
Are great in winter, pleading in mute prayer,
  A dead, drowned face stares up immutably.

The idea of mute prayer is key to Campbell's crisis of faith. In the late Victorian era, Christian dogma was under attack from new scientific discoveries and from the theory of evolution. Even a serious

Anglican like Campbell suffered from the effects of this climate of religious doubt.

Although he read theology at the Episcopal Theological School in Cambridge (Massachusetts) and had been ordained in 1886, Campbell quit the ministry in 1891, after having held ministerial posts with congregations in New Hampshire, New Brunswick, and Ontario. Unlike his fellow Confederation Poet Frederick George Scott, who saw examples of God's goodness and grace in unspoiled nature, Campbell came to suspect that nature more often served as a metaphor for despair, not for our Creator's love. In this, Campbell's break from Victorian and Edwardian Romanticism was profound. And rather Canadian.

As a young man, the poet, much like Charles Sangster, thought he could find in nature an experience of the transcendent much like the transcendent experience found in Christian meditation and prayer. By the advent of the 20th century, he had come to doubt this. What he found in nature was often nature's spirit, not God's. But Campbell's spiritual struggles were not his alone. The 1890s and the early years of the next century were times of widespread religious perplexity and uncertainty.

During 1892 and 1893, Campbell joined with two other Confederation poets, Archibald Lampman and Duncan Campbell Scott, both of whom were, like Campbell, the sons of clergymen, to write a series of pieces for *The Globe* newspaper.[6] Their little essays often discussed the intellectual, cultural, and political issues of the day, and in this way they map the gradual shift away from a traditional classic and Christian view of life under the forceful encroachment of scientific ideas. The movement was away from the rigid acceptance of Church teachings and into a new world of ambiguous and apparently *relative* truths.

In his "The Tragedy of Man" Campbell states clearly his idea concerning the relationship of man to God and of man to nature. While we all might contain a spark of the Divine we also have feet of clay. And these feet of clay prevent us from attaining our God-like potential. This leads unfailingly to strife, sorrow, and death. Absent from "The Tragedy of Man" is any firm assurance of Divine forgiveness or the possibility of salvation, so the fate of man could become a true tragedy. This more severe opinion of humanity is in keeping with his more Spartan, and less romantic, view of the natural world with its focus on winter and winter imagery. Campbell's view of life and the human condition changed over time. During the Victorian era when he published his early books, he was more romantic. He was less so the closer he got to modern times. Because his poem deals with matters of faith and spirituality during the Edwardian period of the early 20th century, a time of questioning and uncertainty, "The Tragedy of Man"[7] rewards close study.

The Tragedy of Man

Long, long ago;
  Ere these material days;
Ere man learned o'er much for the golden glow
  Of Love's divine amaze;
Ere faith was slain; there came to this sad earth
  A high, immortal being of source divine,
And mingling with the upward climbing life,
  Like crystal water in some fevered wine,
Wakened in one red blood mysterious strife,
  Knowledge of good and ill, and that sad birth
  Of splendour and woe for all who yearn and pine.

And this is why,
  Down in the craving, remorseful human heart
There doth remain a dream that will not die,
  All unassuagèd hunger, that o'er the smart
Of sorrow and shame and travail, clamours eterne
For some high goal, some vision of being superne,
  Life doth not grant, earth doth not satisfy.

This is the secret of the heart of man
    And his sad tragedy; his godlike powers;
His summer of vastness, and the wintery ban
    Of all his greatness high which deity dowers,
Sunk to the yearnings of goat-footed Pan;
Hinted of Shakespeare and that mighty clan
Of earth's high prophets, who in their brief day,
    Holding the glory of the god in them,
Though chained to cravings of the lesser clay,
    Dreamed earth's high dreams, and wore love's diadem.

Yea, this is why,
    Through all earth's travail and joy, her seasons brief
Through all her beauty and genius that will not die,
    Surges a mighty grief,
Mingling with our heart's best piety;—
    A sadness, dread, divine,
    Lifting us beyond the pagan wine
And dance of life,
The satyr clamour and strife,
    Unto a dream of being, a yearning flame
    Of that heredity whence our sorrowings came.

This was one of Campbell's favourite pieces, and he valued it highly.

By the time *Beyond the Hills of Dream*[8] was published, nature poems, while still present, had started to be displaced by poems celebrating the Crown, the British Empire, and a strong Canada within the Empire. This volume included poems like "England," glorifying British traditions, and "Victoria," an ode on the Queen's Jubilee in 1897. The title of his final collection of verse, *Sagas of Vaster Britain: Poems of the Race, the Empire and the Divinity of Man*,[9] tells its readers what to expect within its pages. Campbell had journeyed quite some distance from the nature-loving Anglican clergyman of the 1880s, and in this he displayed the social and philosophical trends in early 20th century thought. By the time he edited *The*

Oxford Book of Canadian Verse,[10] it was not his nature poetry he wanted to preserve. Rather, he saw his lasting work as poems like "The Tragedy of Man."

Campbell, coming as he did when Canadian society was changing with the beginnings of Modernism, holds in his literary imagination both the hope for Canada displayed by the Fathers of Confederation in 1867 and what Canada would likely become in the world of shifting values the 20th century offered. He thought that the Monarchy and British traditions would serve as a vital and bracing corrective and ultimately prevent us from slipping into a society devoid of meaning. That is to say, British traditions and the Anglican Church operated for the betterment of mankind. This represented his response to the *fin de siècle* culture that held sway at the close of the 19th century. Campbell's view was, to one degree or another, common among many, but not all, Poets of Confederation.

Despite his effort, Campbell could not hold Modernism at bay, and today he is almost exclusively known for his early nature poetry. Campbell was never shy about his admiration for William Wordsworth, and he took pains to draw a parallel between the English Lake District and the Canadian Lake Region. Nonetheless, their Lake District and our Lake Region are quite different. Here our poet discovered the stern, but good, beauty that lies in the heart of Canada and at the heart of the Canadian spirit. While he may have grown overly pessimistic in his opinion of human nature, he understood the core values of Canada.

During the First World War, Campbell worked as a recruiting officer and served as a drill sergeant with the Home Guard. He died of pneumonia in Ottawa on New Year's Day of 1918, ten months prior to the Armistice. By the time of his death, his verse was being compared to the work of Keats and Shelley. Despite his crisis of faith, Wilfred Campbell was among the few poets in Canada who lived up to the brave ideals of Romanticism, albeit a harsh Romanticism.

Today, Campbell's political and social verse is long out-of-print and nearly forgotten. But nature images from his beloved Lake Region like the following examples will live forever:

Crags that are black and wet out of the grey lake looming,
Under the sunset's flush and the pallid, faint glimmer of dawn;
Shadowy, ghost-like shores, where midnight surfs are booming
Thunders of wintry woe over the spaces wan.

—from "The Winter Lakes"[11]

and

For weeks and weeks the autumn world stood still,
Clothed in the shadow of a smoky haze;
The fields were dead, the wind had lost its will,
And all the lands were hushed by wood and hill,
In those grey, withered days.

—from "How One Winter Came in the Lake Region"[12]

Sophia M. Almon Hensley

Poet of Romance

Sophia (or more often Sophie) M. (Margaretta) Almon Hensley, the youngest of our Confederation Poets, was born in Bridgetown, Nova Scotia on May 31, 1866. Although Canadian by birth, she was educated in England and Paris. For much of her life, Hensley lived in New York, England, and on the British Channel Islands, although she frequently visited Nova Scotia during the summers. Indeed, she counted St. Marys Bay as one of her best-loved spots and often set her poems in her native province, especially along the Bay of Fundy. She enjoyed a long life, retiring to Windsor, Nova Scotia, where she died on February 10, 1946.

"Slack Tide"[1] demonstrates her affection for her Nova Scotian homeland and her precise eye for exacting detail:

Slack Tide

My boat is still in the reedy cove
  Where the rushes hinder its outward course,
For I care not now if we rest or move
  O'er the slumberous tide to the river's source.

My boat is fast in the tall dank weeds,
  And I lay my oars in silence by,
And lean and draw the slippery reeds
  Through my listless fingers carelessly.

The bubbling froth of the surface foam
  Clings close to the side of my moveless boat
Like endless meshes of honeycomb,—
  And I break it off, and send it afloat.

A faint wind stirs, and I drift along
  Far down the stream to its utmost bound,
And the thick white foam-flakes gathering strong,
  Still cling, and follow, and fold around.

Oh! the weary green of the weedy waste,
  The thickening scum of the frothy foam,
And the torpid heart by the reeds embraced
  And shrouded and held in its cheerless home.

The fearful stillness of wearied calm,
  The tired quiet of ended strife,
The echoed note of a heart's sad psalm,
  The sighing end of a wasted life.

The reeds cling close, and my cradle sways,
  And the white gull dips in the waters' barm,
And the heart asleep in the twilight haze
  Feels not its earth-bonds, knows not alarm.

In addition to her poetry of nature, Hensley also was concerned about the erosion of religious belief that was noted during the latter part of the 19th century. While some poets, like her mentor Sir Charles G.D. Roberts, eventually rejected the faith of their fathers, other poets, like Frederick George Scott, were appalled by the questioning of religion. And so was Hensley. Her sonnet "There Is No God"[2] is her response.

There Is No God

There is no God? If one should stand at noon
  Where the glow rests, and the warm sunlight plays,
  Where earth is gladdened by the cordial rays
And blossoms, answering,—where the calm lagoon
Gives back the brightness of the heart of June,
  And he should say, "There is no sun"—the day's
  Fair show still round him,—should we lose the blaze
And warmth, and weep that day has gone so soon?

Nay, there would be one word, one only thought,
  "The man is blind!" and throbs of pitying scorn
    Would rouse the heart, and stir the wondering mind.
  We feel and see, and therefore know,—the morn
With blush of youth ne'er left us till it brought
    Promise of full-grown day. "The man is blind!"

But despite the quality and vividness of her nature poetry, it was not her pastoral verse that established her reputation, as lovely as those poems may be. Hensley is chiefly known today for her love poetry. "When Summer Comes"[3] is a fine example:

When Summer Comes

When summer comes, and when o'er hill and lea
The sun's strong wooing glow hath patiently
  Shed o'er the earth long days his golden dower,
  And then, by force of his own loving power
Drawn the hard frost, and left it passive, free
To give forth all its sweets untiringly,
Shall not the day rise fair for thee and me
  And all life seem but as an opening flower
      When summer comes?

The days move slowly,—young hearts yearn to be
Together always,—cannot brook to see
Their love-days pass, and void each sunny hour;
Yet can we smile e'en when Fate's storm-clouds lower,
Waiting fulfillment of our hearts' decree
When summer comes.

Her poetry was discovered by Sir Charles G.D. Roberts during the late 1880s while she was still a young writer, and prior to her marriage to Halifax lawyer Hubert Hensley. Roberts promoted her work to various editors and publishers, which helped quickly launch her career. She was an early and lifelong feminist who believed the power of love would ultimately bring women and men together and heal the wounds of sexism. Indeed, though born a Victorian woman, to the degree possible she lived the life of a modern woman.[4]

And like other women covered by this study, Hensley worried about the wear and tear of the passing years. As a woman who lived for romance, this was a concern; the poet lived to be seventy-nine years old. In writing about the dream of youth, she said:[5]

Song

Joy came in youth as a humming-bird,
(Sing hey! for the honey and bloom of life!)
And it made a home in my summer bower
With the honeysuckle and the sweet-pea flower.
(Sing hey! for the blossoms and sweets of life!)

Joy came as a lark when the years had gone,
(Ah! hush, hush still, for the dream is short!)
And I gazed far up to the melting blue
Where the rare song dropped like a golden dew.
(Ah! sweet is the song tho' the dream be short!)

Joy hovers now in a far-off mist,
  (The night draws on and the air breathes snow!)
And I reach, sometimes, with a trembling hand
To the red-tipped cloud of the joy-bird's land.
  (Alas! for the days of the storm and the snow!)

The fact that editors like Carole Gerson and Gwendolyn Davies consider poets such as Susan Frances Harrison, Helena Coleman, and Sophia M. Almon Hensley to be secondary, or minor, poets, and editors like Jack David and Robert Lecker[6] and Margaret Atwood[7] consider them not at all, does not mean contemporary readers should ignore their poetry. During the 19th century and well past the midpoint of the 20th century, it was all too common for female writers to be overlooked or underappreciated, especially in the field of poetry. Nonetheless, Harrison, Coleman, and Hensley helped shape Canada as their nation emerged from colonization. Their vision of Canada was much like that of their male counterparts: an English-language country that, while cherishing its roots in British and Irish culture, was independent within what is now the Commonwealth, and that was Christian in nature, religion being vital in the lives of its people.

Hensley, very much the disciple of Sir Charles G.D. Roberts, was likewise influenced by British poets of the Victorian Period, whom she studied while a student at St. Monica's School in Warwickshire, England. This tended to give her poetry an "English" flavour.

It is worth keeping in mind that four of our Confederation Poets—Hensley, Duncan Campbell Scott, Helena Coleman, and William Douw Lighthall—lived through World War I, the Great Depression, and World War II. They may be viewed as writers of the Confederation Period as well as writers of 20th century Modernism in poetry, as represented by T.S. Eliot and Ezra Pound.[8] They formed the bridge between the old Canada of Charles Sangster and the new Canada of Al Purdy and Raymond Souster.[9]

John Frederic Herbin

Poet of the Acadian Diaspora

On June 24, 1893, in the final piece he would write for the "At The Mermaid Inn" feature in *The Globe*, Archibald Lampman alerted the readers of that Toronto newspaper to the arrival of a new poet. Lampman wrote: "... there seems to me high and serious tone in this little collection of poems. I think it is the tone of one who loves beauty, and loves her purely and honestly."[1] Lampman went so far as to quote a poem in its entirety. The poet in question was John Frederic Herbin, the book was *The Marshlands*, and the sonnet Lampman shared with the readers of *The Globe* was "Haying."

Herbin is unique among our poets of the Confederation Period in that he was an Acadian who wrote in English.[2] In fact, our poet would go on to publish such prose works, mostly non-fiction, as *Grand-Pré: A Sketch of the Acadian Occupation of the Shores of the Basin of Minas*, *The History of Grand-Pré: The Home of Longfellow's "Evangeline," The Heir to Grand-Pré* (fiction), and *The Land of Evangeline: The Authentic Story of Her Country and Her People*, all in English. He was the major historian of the Acadian People of the Grand-Pré/Minas Basin region of Nova Scotia.

Herbin's main topic was the Acadian Diaspora.[3] This lasted for eight years (1755–1763). Some ten thousand Acadians were deported from the Bay of Fundy area. Conditions were so dire that half of them died of disease or starvation. Villages were put to the torch, churches destroyed. An attempt was made to wipe out the Acadian culture: an 18th century version of ethnic cleansing. Nonetheless, a few Acadians escaped deportation by fleeing to what is now New Brunswick.

The Canadian government chose to ignore this stain on our

history. Although our poet was born a century after these tragic events—he lived from February 8, 1860 to December 20, 1923—the suffering of his people seemed to him to be much more recent, much more vivid and crucial. The opening two stanzas of the title poem of his book show how he was "called" by the spirits of the dead and of the land they farmed to recapture and retell this history:[4]

The Marshlands

Oh, dykes that are mourning a nation
    That laid you and lifted you high;
Ye fields with your old lamentation
    And the grief that shall live with the sky,

I have found me adrift on your meadows,
    And hailed by the voice of the deep,
As if called from the region of shadows,
    Or waked from the vision of sleep.

In fact, at the same time Bliss Carman was writing his famous poem "Low Tide on Grand Pré," Herbin, the Acadian, was writing this:[5]

An Acadian at Grand-Pré

To-day, alone of all my scattered race,
    I see again the beauty of our land,
    Made fair and fruitful by a banished hand;
Made sweet of tongue, now with no biding-place.
And Nature has remembered, for a trace
    Of calm Acadian life yet holds command,
    Where undisturbed the rustling willows stand,
And the curved grass, telling the breeze's pace.
Before the march of power the weak must bend,
    And yet forgive; the savage strong will smite.
        The glossing words of reason and of song,

To tell of hate and virtue to defend,
    Shall never set the bitter deed aright,
        Nor satisfy the ages with the wrong.

Having become the voice of his people, Herbin could bring history back to life in poems like "The Gaspereau":[6]

The Gaspereau

Below me winds the river to the sea,
    On whose brown slope stood wailing, homeless maids;
    Stood exiled sons; unsheltered hoary heads;
And sires and mothers dumb in agony.
The awful glare of burning homes, where free
    And happy late they dwelt, breaks on the shades
    Encompassing the sailing fleet; then fades
With tumbling roof upon the night-bound sea.
How deep is hope in sorrow sunk! How harsh
    The stranger voice; and loud the hopeless wail!
        Then silence came to dwell; the tide fell low;
The embers died. On the deserted marsh,
    Where grain and grass stirred only to the gale,
        The moose unchased dare cross the Gaspereau.

Indeed, the two ideas Herbin wanted to leave with his readers were the extent of the crime committed against his ancestors and the natural beauty of Grand-Pré in particular and of the entire Minas Basin in general. He was born in Windsor, Nova Scotia, and spent his adult life in Wolfville, where he had graduated from Acadia College, now Acadia University. Wolfville is quite near the old Acadian village of Grand-Pré. Herbin was a founder of Evangeline Park and was the guiding light behind the ultimate establishment of the Grand-Pré National Historic Site, today a UNESCO World Heritage Site. His contributions to Canadian history, and to our understanding of that history, cast a large shadow.

But Herbin is presented here as a poet, not as a historian. In his aforementioned book review of *The Marshlands*, Archibald Lampman wrote: "Mr Herbin is a landscape painter in verse, and he has the power to paint landscape admirably—sometimes singularly—well." In this, Herbin is like Bliss Carman, who, as noted, also wrote of Grand-Pré, and Sir Charles G.D. Roberts, with whom he corresponded. Our poet felt a kinship with both Roberts and Carman, as evidenced by his poem "To The Singers of Minas"[7] in *The Marshlands*. Of Roberts, Herbin wrote:

> The broad green plain of level Tantramar
> Is but the Tempe of thy ancient time.
> The tides, and all the Fundean crystal ways
> Live as thy blue Ægean was in far
> Dim yesterdays ...

And of Carman, he wrote:

> And in thy wandering voices call to thee
> Sad with remembrance of the deathless wrong.
> And thou art in the circle of the few
> Who tune their voices to these singing meads,
> And know the assonance of shore and tide,
> And the swift stroke of wavelet slipping through
> The grasses; learning from the river reeds
> The deepest chorus of the ocean wide.

In the case of these three poets of the Bay of Fundy, it is hardly possible to separate the landscape from the poets who grew up there. And although Carman and Roberts are both English-Canadians and Herbin is Acadian, our poet finds true brotherhood in a united Canada:

And here has love uprisen into song,
And filled our souls with yearning and the glow
Of deathless life. Where was that hate of yore
That made our fathers foemen, now grows strong
The peace of nationhood, although the flow
Of tears has marked the whole red reach of shore.

The very nature of day-to-day human lives in this region, and the rhythms of their work, are controlled by the seasons and the massive Fundy tides. Here one finds many sea meadows that are slightly under water part of every day, and a great deal of hay is grown in these sea-washed fields. This is made clear in the poem Lampman quoted in his review in which this sea-scented hay is harvested for fodder:[8]

Haying

From the soft dyke-road, crooked and wagon-worn,
Comes the great load of rustling scented hay,
Slow-drawn with heavy swing and creaky sway
Through the cool freshness of the windless morn.
The oxen, yoked and sturdy, horn to horn,
Sharing the rest and toil of night and day,
Bend head and neck to the long hilly way
By many a season's labor marked and torn.
On the broad sea of dyke the gathering heat
Waves upward from the grass, where road on road
Is swept before the tramping of the teams.
And while the oxen rest beside the sweet
New hay, the loft receives the early load,
With hissing stir, among the dusty beams.

Despite Herbin's obvious importance to the Acadian People and their culture, and despite the quality of his own poetry, after his death in 1923, he was forgotten for several decades until Professor

Gwendolyn Davies of Acadia University revived his reputation a quarter of a century ago. While Carman and Roberts left the Fundy area to live outside Canada, Herbin remained at home writing about the land he loved. Unlike any other major writer of his time, Herbin is totally regional. Almost every book he wrote, and almost every poem, is set in the Minas Basin, an area of outstanding natural beauty. Herbin's devotion to his people left the Grand-Pré National Historic Site as a permanent marker on the physical geography of Canada; likewise, his poetry should have a lasting home in Canadian literature.

Susan Frances Harrison

The Poet who Looked to Québec

Widely read in her time, and perhaps among the few Confederation women read today, was Susan Frances Harrison, who quite often used the *nom de plume* Seranus. Our poet was a Torontonian through and through, having been born in that city on February 24, 1859 and dying there at age seventy-six on May 5, 1935. But she studied for a couple of years in Montréal, where she developed a keen interest in Québécois literature, and this experience coloured much of her stance toward Canadian literature. She returned to Toronto after living for a few years in Ottawa, her first book having been published in Canada's capital. During her Toronto-based journalistic career, Harrison wrote for *The Globe* (forerunner of *The Globe and Mail*), the (Detroit) *Free Press*, and *The Week*, where she briefly served as editor.

Harrison's initial publication was a collection of stories, *Crowded Out! And Other Sketches*[1] (1886). Harrison was influenced by the work of Edgar Allan Poe, both for her fiction and for her poetry. Her début collection of verse, *Pine, Rose, and Fleur de Lis*,[2] from which the following poem is quoted, appeared five years later in 1891. Both her poetry and her fiction display her lasting interest in Québec and Québec's culture. In her poetry, she had a love for the sonnet and, especially, the villanelle. A typical poem is "*Les Chantiers*."[3]

Les Chantiers

For know, my girl, there is always the axe
    Ready at hand in this latitude,
And how it stings and bites and hacks

When Alphonse the sturdy trees attacks!
    So fear, child, to cross him, or play the prude,
For know, my girl, there is always the axe.

See! it shines even now as his hands relax
    Their grip with a dread desire imbu'd,
And how it stings and bites and hacks,

And how it rips and cuts and cracks
    —Perhaps—in his brain as the foe is pursu'd,
For know, my girl, there is always the axe.

The giant boles in the forest tracks
    Stagger, soul-smitten, when afar it is view'd,
And how it stings and bites and hacks!

Then how, Madelon, should its fearful thwacks
    A slender lad like your own elude?
For know, my girl, there is always the axe,
And how it stings! and bites! and hacks!

Not only is this a villanelle set in French Canada, it also displays Poe's somewhat macabre sensibility.

Another villanelle set in Québec that shows her interest in French culture and history is "Château Papineau"[4] in celebration of Louis-Joseph Papineau.[5]

Château Papineau

The red til'd towers of the old Château,
    Perch'd on the cliff above our bark,
Burn in the western evening glow.

The fiery spirit of Papineau
    Consumes them still with its fever spark,
The red til'd towers of the old Château!

Drift by and mark how bright they show,
    And how the mullion'd windows—mark!
Burn in the western evening glow!

Drift down, or up, where'er you go,
    They flame from out the distant park,
The red til'd towers of the old Château.

So was it once with friend, with foe;
    Far off they saw the patriot's ark
Burn in the western evening glow.

Think of him now! One thought bestow,
    As, blazing against the pine trees dark,
The red til'd towers of the old Château
Burn in the western evening glow!

Although Harrison's life was as urban as one could be, living in cities from birth to death, like other Confederation Poets she celebrated the natural landscape of Canada, and our dominant season of winter. Her sonnet "Niagara in Winter"[6] is one example. Any reader who has visited Niagara Falls in January will know this scene.

Niagara in Winter

Nor similes nor metaphors avail!
All imagery vanishes, device
Dies in thy presence, wondrous dream of ice!
Ice-bound I stand, my face is pinched and pale,
Before such awful majesty I fail,
Sink low on this snow-lichened slab of gneiss,
Shut out the gleaming mass that can entice,
Enchain, enchant, but in whose light I quail.

While I from under frozen lashes peer,
My thoughts fly back and take a homeward course.
How dear to dwell in sweet placidity,
Instead of these colossal crystals, see
The slender icicles of some fairy "force,"
And break the film upon an English mere!

She also wrote about aging, relating the seasons of a woman's life to the seasons of the year. But unlike the natural year, which repeats itself as spring follows winter, for people youth never returns.

September

I

Birds that were gray in the green are black in the yellow.
Here where the green remains rocks one little fellow.

Quaker in gray, do you know that the green is going?
More than that—do you know that the yellow is showing?

II

Singer of songs, do you know that your Youth is flying?
That Age will soon at the lock of your life be prying?

Lover of life, do you know that the brown is going?
More than that—do you know that the gray is showing?[7]

Harrison was a major figure in her day. Her journalism influenced public opinion, especially on cultural matters. This was important in an era in which writers and artists were attempting to "define" Canada. She wrote six volumes of poetry, two novels, various articles and lectures, a book of short stories, and composed music. She valued her Irish roots—her maiden name was Riley—and wrote a

"String Quartet on Ancient Irish Airs" as well as piano versions of traditional French-Canadian airs in honour of her Irish heritage and her love of Québec culture.

Bliss Carman

Poet of Transcendentalism

Although born in Fredericton, New Brunswick on April 15, 1861, William Bliss Carman was the most American of our Confederation Poets. Carman spent almost all of his adult life outside Canada, mostly in the United States, and lived in New Canaan, Connecticut for his final twenty-one years. He died in New Canaan on June 8, 1929, but at his request, his remains were returned to Fredericton, where he is buried. While Carman was of United Empire Loyalist stock, a group who rejected the revolutionary liberalism of the United States, he greatly admired the Americans, publishing mostly in the U.S., and appears as an American poet in two important books. In 1904 Jessie B. Rittenhouse published *The Younger American Poets*[1] and in 1919 Louis Untermeyer's seminal *Modern American Poetry: A Critical Anthology*[2] appeared. Both studies treat Carman as one of the newer, and more interesting, if a tad regional, of the American poets.

Like most Canadian poets of his time, Carman was influenced by the work of such late British Victorians as Alfred, Lord Tennyson and Robert Browning, but he was much more attracted to the writings of Ralph Waldo Emerson and Henry David Thoreau. Indeed, Carman and Emerson (1803–1882) were distant cousins.[3] He especially liked Emerson's essays *Nature*[4] and "Self-Reliance"[5] and, like Emerson, he soon divested himself of Christianity, taking up American Transcendentalism.

The question arises: What qualifies Bliss Carman as a major Canadian Confederation Poet if he was largely American? There are two chief reasons for this. First, as Professor Terry Whalen of Saint Mary's University has noted, the high point of Confederation culture was from the 1880s to the First World War, a period of three and a half decades.[6] Carman, like his first cousin Sir Charles G.D. Roberts, did his best work in poetry early, that is, prior to the Great War. Although all of Carman's poetry collections contain fine poems, he is mainly known today for the poetry he published during the 1890s, and the setting of these early poems is often the land where he grew up. (Examples of this point are "Why," "A Windflower," "In Lyric Season," "At the Voice of a Bird," "Carnations in Winter," and "In Apple Time," all from his first poetry collection.) Second, after 1920 Carman began to publish in Canada via McClelland & Stewart and the Ryerson Press. And, although he continued to reside in Connecticut, he presented a few reading/lecture tours in his homeland. He clearly wished to maintain a Canadian connection.

The first of these points is quite important for our examination of Canadian culture. Along with Bliss Carman, several Confederation Poets lived well into the post-war period: Susan Frances Harrison died in 1935, Agnes Ethelwyn Wetherald in 1940, Sir Charles G.D. Roberts in 1943, Frederick George Scott in 1944, Sophia Almon Hensley in 1946, Duncan Campbell Scott in 1947, Helena Coleman lived until 1953, and William Douw Lighthall made it to 1954. It was no longer the 19th century, and the Canada they grew to adulthood in had been swept away by the forces of war and Modernism.[7] The Victorian and Edwardian culture of the young Canada these poets both represented and helped establish, and that Carman still clung to, had been replaced by T.S. Eliot and Ezra Pound. More than anything else, the war had dragged Canada into an industrialized urban society made ever more powerful by the gravitational attraction of the United States and, to a lesser degree, Great Britain. All of our poets who continued into the post-war period had to adjust as best they could. But this new world was not the world of Bliss Carman; it was a world he would never accept.

To return to the young poet and his early days, in Fredericton Bliss Carman attended first the Fredericton Collegiate School, as did his cousins Barry Bliss Straton and Sir Charles G.D. Roberts, and later he went to the University of New Brunswick (B.A. 1881, M.A. 1884). Between these two degrees he studied in Britain at Oxford

University and the University of Edinburgh. He then was at Harvard University from 1886 to 1888, where his thought was influenced by the ideas of George Santayana, and Josiah Royce, the philosopher who established American objective idealism. It was in the United States that Carman developed his life-long interest in Transcendentalism.

It strikes me as odd that a young Canadian would take up Transcendentalism in the late 1880s when the movement had pretty much expired in the U.S. Emerson, Thoreau, Margaret Fuller, Orestes Brownson, and Jones Very were all dead. And Brook Farm had closed in 1847, long before Carman had been born. By the early years of the 20th century, Carman might have been the only Transcendentalist actively publishing books. But then, in many respects, Carman never really left the 19th century.

In addition to writing philosophical verse from a mystical Transcendentalist perspective, and later from a rigid Delsartean unitrinian[8] point of view, Carman was an excellent poet of nature. Much of Carman's nature poetry harkens back to his youthful Maritime concerns and landscapes of the Annapolis Valley. (This, despite his living inland for most of his adult life.) As with many of his fellow Confederation Poets, it is his nature poetry that is best remembered today. It is difficult to believe that his Delsartean unitrinianism is read today.

While a student at Harvard, Carman met a Dr. and Mrs. King of New Canaan, Connecticut. He soon fell in love with Mrs. King and eventually she became his lover.[9] Carman moved to live near the Kings in New Canaan. It was Mary Perry King who introduced our poet to Delsartean unitrinianism, a theory she had learned from the poet Richard Hovey's[10] wife, who had studied in France under Delsarte. Carman and Mary Perry King eventually co-authored a couple of books[11] based on the thought of François Alexandre Nicolas Chéri Delsarte. The Hoveys, Mary Perry King, and Bliss Carman formed a unit of four likeminded people, and they influenced each other's work. It is not, however, King's and Carman's Delsartean æsthetic that concerns us here. It was Transcendentalism that set the tone for much of the poet's later work.

There are almost as many types of Transcendentalism as there are followers. To understand Carman's version, it is useful to consider what Yale University's Professor Odell Shepard had to say. Carman "has the Transcendental belief in the essential identity of man's soul with the Soul of the universe, the belief in man's consequent kinship with Nature, and finally the reliance upon intuition as the means whereby man becomes aware in ecstatic moments of his mystical union with the Over-soul."[12] It might be said that both Emerson and Carman embraced non-Christian Transcendentalism as a reaction to, or rejection of, their strict Puritan ancestry.

Unlike Emerson, Carman's Transcendentalism, strong as it might have been, was tinged with Loyalist (Church of England) ideas. His native New Brunswick had been established by the United Empire Loyalists, and Carman came of Loyalist stock. This blend of Church of England, Puritan, and Transcendentalist ideas helped make Carman's poetry unique, and rather Canadian. Perhaps it would be more useful to consider Carman to have been a believer in neo-Transcendentalism, something of his own invention, rather than in the orthodox version found in the writings of Emerson and Thoreau.

Aside from Carman's widely-anthologized poem "Low Tide on Grand Pré,"[13] another key work that illustrates his poetry at its best is "A Vagabond Song":[14]

A Vagabond Song

There is something in the autumn that is native to my
    blood—
Touch of manner, hint of mood;
And my heart is like a rhyme,
With the yellow and the purple and the crimson keeping time.

The scarlet of the maples can shake me like a cry
Of bugles going by.
And my lonely spirit thrills
To see the frosty asters like a smoke upon the hills.

There is something in October sets the gypsy blood astir;
We must rise and follow her,
When from every hill of flame
She calls and calls each vagabond by name.

It is clear that here we have a poet of moods, feelings, and emotions, not a purveyor of formal ideas or philosophical concepts. Or, in the poet's own words: "The essence of religion is emotion, not the thought—the sure and certain conviction, not the logical conclusion."[15] This is most deftly expressed in his nature poetry and in his love poetry. These together could qualify Carman as a neo-Romantic in the minds of some readers. Carman continued in this vein until his final poetry collection in 1929, the year he died. Here is the first sonnet from his short series "The Winter Scene."[16] (Oddly enough, the other three sonnets in this series are 14-line poems, but the opening sonnet is only a 13-line poem.)

The Winter Scene

The rutted roads are all like iron; skies
Are keen and brilliant; only the oak-leaves cling
In the bare woods, or the hardy bitter-sweet;
Drivers have put their sheepskin jackets on;
And all the ponds are sealed with sheeted ice
That rings with stroke of skate and hockey-stick,
Or in the twilight cracks with running whoop.
Bring in the logs of oak and hickory,
And make an ample blaze on the wide hearth.
Now is the time, with winter o'er the world,
For books and friends and yellow candle-light,
And timeless lingering by the settling fire.
While all the shuddering stars are keen with cold.

When they were confronted with the modern world the First World War engendered, some Confederation Poets, like Duncan Campbell Scott, embraced certain modernist literary concepts. They adapted, and they eventually accepted the world as they found it, uncongenial as it might have been to them. Other poets, like Frederick George Scott, acknowledged their changed circumstances, but forcefully resisted modernist ideas. Bliss Carman elected to ignore the 20th century entirely. He happily withdrew to his pretty colonial town of New Canaan, in those days very much off the beaten path, as if the World War had never happened.

But Canada could not simply withdraw into its more innocent and pastoral past; in truth, Canada would never be the same. Although Wilfred Campbell could not know it, the country and culture he had written about so confidently on the eve of the Great War when he introduced *The Oxford Book of Canadian Verse* was about to end. English-speaking Canada in the latter decades of the 19th century was, he thought, a conservative, Christian society that would certainly grow during the 20th century into a mature nation based firmly on "British ideals, traditions, religion, history, and heredity."[17] Due to circumstances beyond the control of any group of poets, the Canada of 1913 was soon to become a liberal, commercial, secular nation more strongly connected to the United States than to jolly old England. At the time of his death, Bliss Carman was a Canadian poet harbouring a strikingly Victorian point of view living, not just in the wrong country, but also in the wrong century.

Duncan Campbell Scott:
Poet of the Canadian Shield

Writing in 1960, Malcolm Ross observed that the Confederation Poets "were avowed and self-conscious prophets of the new Canadian nationalism."[1] Ross goes on to add that "This was a nationalism in search of a nation ..."[2] More than any other 19th century poet, Duncan Campbell Scott found that nation in the land between the Great Lakes and Hudson Bay.

Duncan Campbell Scott, the son of a Methodist minister, was born in Ottawa on August 2, 1862. During his long life Scott lived to see World War I, the Great Depression, and World War II. He died on December 19, 1947 at age eighty-five. For the main part, Scott grew up in various small communities throughout rural Québec and Ontario as his father moved from village to village. Unlike most of his fellow Confederation Poets, Scott did not attend university; his family was too poor, and he left school early. From age seventeen until he retired in 1932, he was employed by the federal Department of Indian Affairs. He started as a lowly clerk and ended up as the Deputy Superintendent General of Indian Affairs.

The most important poetry Scott wrote is a direct result of his work at Indian Affairs. While Scott addressed many topics, including love poetry, nature poetry, and poems of his Christian faith, he is known today for his poems dealing with Indigenous people and with the geography and raw beauty of the Canadian Shield. His job involved much travel to remote First Nations communities and this brought him into direct and extensive contact with northern Ontario. During the course of Scott's work at Indian Affairs, he was notably the chief federal negotiator for Treaty No. 9.[3] This treaty took place in 1905 between the Cree and the Ojibwa of northern Ontario and the Ontario and Canadian governments. The effect of this treaty was to dispossess the Cree and Ojibwa of most of their land.

Scott was also involved in the administration of the Residential Schools. Renewed interest in these schools was sparked in the spring of 2021 when thousands of unmarked and unrecorded graves of Indigenous children were discovered on the grounds of some of the former schools. In 1909 Scott said the goal of these schools "includes not only a scholastic education, but instruction in the means of gaining a livelihood from the soil or as a member of an industrial or mercantile community, and the substitution of Christian ideals of conduct and morals for aboriginal concepts of both."[4] Of note here is the goal of Christianizing Indigenous children as part of the "educational" process the Canadian government established. Therefore, these schools were operated by Christian churches.

Because he directly interacted with them, it is probably true that Scott understood the different Indigenous Peoples of northern Ontario and their cultures better than most other White men of his time. And, just as important, he understood the land of Canada, especially the land north of Lake Superior. Like the people who had lived here for thousands of years, the poet came to believe that Canada had a given nature or spirit largely independent of human activity, and thus Canada had a *meaning*. In his view, this meaning was expressed most clearly by the Canadian (or Precambrian) Shield, a geological feature dominating much of Ontario and Québec, the old, or original, Upper and Lower Canada. It must be kept in mind that as a leading writer of his era, Scott's depictions of Indigenous Peoples and their various cultures in his poetry and prose—however accurate or inaccurate his depictions might have been—was both indicative of, and influential towards, how they were being perceived and treated by the broader populace.

His poetry about the Indigenous Peoples was anticipated by the poetry of Isabella Valancy Crawford. Crawford held an innocent and even a romantic view of these First Canadians and their culture. Unlike Crawford, Scott's thoughts concerning the tribes he interacted with were complex. Indeed, they were deeply conflicted.[5]

Crawford's view represents the 19th century's more naïve version of Romanticism—she died in 1887, six years before Scott published his first poetry collection—while Scott was dealing with an ugly 20th century reality. Although many people held a positive view of the relationship between the First Nations and the Canadian government in Crawford's day, the sad reality of how the marginalization of Indigenous communities was progressing had become painfully clear by the time Scott was writing his best-known poetry.

While Scott's friend and colleague Wilfred Campbell privileged verse that upheld the "British ideals, traditions, religion, history, and heredity"[6] of the men and women who established English-speaking Canada, Scott generally opposed this view. In Scott's opinion, it was a mistake to view Canada through the lens of British or European culture. Canada, while some like Campbell might consider it to form part of a "vaster Britain," was not Britain. Canada was Canada. If White settlers failed to properly "see" Canada, they would be unable to be at rest here. In this, Scott anticipates the poetry of Al Purdy, who said of the Canadian Shield: "This is the country of our defeat"[7] and that his people (Purdy came from United Empire Loyalist stock) had failed to become true Canadians. In Purdy's view, the settlers were never "at home"— or as Scott might say, "at rest"—here. They could not fit in.

A comparison between Scott and Purdy is interesting. Both wrote about the relationship between the Canadian Shield and the settlers who attempted to come to terms with this unfamiliar and harshly beautiful land. Both visited the far north and wrote about its meaning. Scott went to James Bay and Purdy to Baffin Island in the Arctic. And the two poets overlapped with Purdy's initial collection, *The Enchanted Echo*, being published in 1944 and Scott's final volume of mixed prose and verse, *The Circle of Affection*, appearing three years later in 1947.

Scott thought that the Indigenous Peoples of the Shield region were fully at home in Canada because their culture was proper for their land. Scott believed we could learn valuable lessons from these true Canadians while recognizing the sad reality that their fate was to become, in most cases, assimilated into White culture.[8] Despite the heated debate concerning Scott's work at Indian Affairs, especially his directorship of Canada's Residential Schools and his failure to provide adequate health care to Indigenous Peoples,[9] a debate that demands more space than this study can afford, the poet did, like Charles Sangster before him, direct our attention to the Canadian Shield as a place of vital spiritual importance, a view Scott shared with the Cree and Ojibwa of the region.[10]

It is the opinion of critic Gordon Johnston that Scott's poem "The Height of Land" represents "the high point of Scott's poetic career for a number of reasons."[11] In his role as the commissioner of Treaty No. 9, Scott travelled throughout the area between Lake Superior and James Bay meeting with scattered Indigenous groups. The height of land referred to in his poem is that watershed where water on the southern slope flows south into the Great Lakes and water on the northern slope flows north towards James Bay/Hudson Bay and the Arctic Ocean. This was a region few White people visited, especially as early as 1905. Scott was greatly impressed and the course of his best poetry was determined.

Scott's belief in the importance of the land north of Superior, and the poems he set there, foreshadowed the mystical/symbolic landscapes of his friend Lawren Harris. Scott also foreshadowed the Canadian Shield paintings of Tom Thomson especially and by Harris' fellow Group of Seven members in general. These early 20th century artists[12] shared his view that the rugged Shield held a special significance for Canada, that the north was essential to understanding what Canada was and what Canada could become. This was their True North. While Scott visited the region in 1905, Harris discovered the north shore of Lake Superior in 1921. He would return to the region annually for several years, and eventually, like Al Purdy, Harris went as far north as the Arctic.

Very much like the experience of Sangster on his journey up the Saguenay River in 1853, for Scott, entering the north also led to a religious revelation.[13] His most extensive trips throughout northern Ontario were made during 1905 and 1906. These left a lasting impression on the poet's mind and on his understanding of Canada. In "The Height of Land"[14] the poet notes:

> Here there is peace in the lofty air,
> And Something comes by flashes
> Deeper than peace;—
> The spruces have retired a little space
> And left a field of sky in violet shadow
> With stars like marigolds in a water-meadow.[15]

Scott then contrasts the north where he finds "A rocky islet followed/ With one lone poplar ..." in this "lonely north enlaced with lakes" to "The crowded southern land/ With all the welter of the lives of men" where he lives and has recently travelled from. And once again:

> But here is peace, and again
> That Something comes by flashes
> Deeper than peace,—a spell
> Golden and inappellable
> That gives the inarticulate part
> Of our strange being one moment of release
> That seems more native than the touch of time,[16]

The poet affirms that "here, where we can think, on the bright uplands/ Where the air is clear, we deeply brood on life." Then that strange "Something" returns:

> A Something to be guided by ideals—
> That in themselves are simple and serene—
> Of noble deed to foster noble thought,
> And noble thought to image noble deed,
> Till deed and thought shall interpenetrate,
> Making life lovelier ...[17]

Scott has made his poem a long one, a full nine pages in the George H. Doran edition. And yet by the close of his poem this "Something" remains "golden and inappellable." The poet simply cannot depict it clearly. Nonetheless, having contemplated the vast and spreading Shield, the poet finds a deeper meaning. He asks "Shall he base his flight/ Upon a more compelling law than Love/ As Life's atonement … ?" And again, "Shall he stand/ With deeper joy, with more complex emotion,/ In closer commune with divinity … ?"

By the poem's climax, the poet stands "with heart entranced and burning/ At the zenith of our wisdom" and feels "The long light flow, the long wind pause, the deep/ Influx of spirit …" but the "Secret" that animates his experience must always remain "golden and inappellable."

The most anthologized of Scott's major poems often relate to the Indigenous Peoples and the north. These include "The Forsaken," "On the Way to the Mission," "The Onondaga Madonna," "The Half-Breed Girl," and "Powassan's Drum," to mention only a few.

It can be said that no other poet wrote such powerful poems dealing with the brutal treatment of the Native People, not even Pauline Johnson. In "On the Way to the Mission"[18] a Montagnias trapper is taking his wife's body to a mission for Christian burial. The trapper is tracked by two White men who, intent on robbery, shoot and kill him.

In Canada there are a great many people of mixed ancestry. In "The Half-Breed Girl"[19] the protagonist is torn between her father's (White) and her mother's (Native) heritage. Scott tells his reader that "Her dreams are undiscovered" and that she cannot rest. On the one hand are the "rock-built cities" of her father's people while on the other hand is the "stifling wigwam" where she lives. Being neither White nor Indigenous, "Her heart is shaken with longing … For what she knows and knows not."

In Scott's sonnet "The Onondaga Madonna"[20] the baby "sulks" and is "burdened" by his "infant gloom." Like the "Half-Breed Girl," the baby "will not rest." The baby and his mother (the Madonna figure) are members of a "waning race." In a chilling statement, this tiny boy is presented as "The latest promise of her nation's doom" rather than as the hopeful promise of a happy future. Clearly, the child of this Onondaga woman will have no future. (Scott suggests that the father of the baby is White because the child is paler than his mother.) This piece is representative of Scott's poetry on the Indigenous People; here is the poem:

The Onondaga Madonna

She stands full-throated and with careless pose,
This woman of a weird and waning race,
The tragic savage lurking in her face,
Where all her pagan passion burns and glows;
Her blood is mingled with her ancient foes,
And thrills with war and wildness in her veins;
Her rebel lips are dabbled with the stains
Of feuds and forays and her father's woes.

And closer in the shawl about her breast,
The latest promise of her nation's doom,
Paler than she her baby clings and lies,
The primal warrior gleaming from his eyes;
He sulks, and burdened with his infant gloom,
He draws his heavy brows and will not rest.

What this sonnet also points to is the racism and chauvinism inherent in the poet's own views concerning this Onondaga woman. He viewed the coming to the Americas of people from Spain, France, and England as a good thing, perhaps an example of Divine providence. As a Christian, Scott seemed to believe, or even expect, that these original Canadians would have to convert to Christianity and White values or they could not survive. Although the Indigenous culture and religion might have served them well in pre-settlement Canada, that Canada was coming to an end as settlements expanded. In the face of the modern world, it would be either assimilation or eradication. And despite his personal hopes for a "good" result from the treaty process launched by the federal government, a process of which he played a large part, Scott thought survival would be unlikely. In the end these people would face tragedy.

In Scott's most famous piece, "The Forsaken,"[21] the reader is presented with a tightly written opening section in short, staccato, noun-terminated lines that heighten the drama and desperation of the scene. These lines work through rhythm patterns, rather than strict or formal metre. As is customary with the poet's finest work, the setting is the northland and the season is winter. A Chippewa woman and her baby are alone and hungry on a frozen lake a three-day journey from the nearest fort. Unable to catch fish with a naked hook, she finally baits her hook with pieces cut from her own flesh. She catches a pair of trout through the ice and in this way secures enough food so she and her child can reach the fort and safety.

Scott dramatically changes his prosody in his poem's second section, introducing a much longer, freer, and vaguely cadential line. Many years have passed and the woman has become "old and withered." The baby boy she once saved by cutting pieces of her own flesh to catch the trout is now an old man himself, and her grandchildren are filled with vigour. Once more she finds herself on a northern lake with winter coming on. "Because she was old and useless,/ Like a paddle broken and warped" her family abandons her to her fate. They slip off silently and the elderly woman sits and stoically awaits death. As before, three days pass. On the third day a snowstorm covers her "with a beautiful crystal shroud" and she is "gathered up by the hand of God."

Wisely, this poem is written without direct editorial comment from the poet. Readers might suspect that Scott is appalled by this treatment of the elderly, perhaps because they also are shocked. But Scott simply, and brilliantly, tells his story in verse. He achieves an emotional level that is at once universal and tragic.

Scott was a man of his era, and he shared many of its racist attitudes. As a Christian, he viewed the Indigenous People as pagans who should be converted. What set Scott apart from most poets was that, as Gordon Johnston noted, "his attempt to see the Indians as themselves, and not as merely decorative or illustrative," marked "the beginning of an extensive interest in the natives in later poets."[22] That is to say, he worked to avoid projecting White values and clichés on First Nations people. In this Scott's precursor was Isabella Valancy Crawford, although it is not known how familiar he might have been with her work. The key is that Scott thought the Indigenous Peoples had developed a spiritual understanding of, or bond with, Canada, especially those tribes based on the Canadian Shield, that was not commonly shared by the European and British settlers coming into northern Québec and Ontario. After all, White Canadians were relative newcomers while the Indigenous tribes had been living here for over ten thousand years. This northernness truly set Scott apart for, although both Frederick George Scott in Québec and Wilfred Campbell in Ontario celebrated the Canadian Shield in their verse, their commitment to the north was less focused, less mystical.

Scott was torn by the conflict between the Old World culture (Britain) and the raw New World (Canada). He was deeply moved by the poetry and literary tradition of English masters like Matthew Arnold and Alfred, Lord Tennyson. But he was also inspired by the Canadian poetry of his friends Archibald Lampman and Wilfred Campbell. He was keenly aware of the conflict between the increasingly urban and industrial south and the still largely wild northland. Finally, there was a clear, and painful, conflict between Scott's Christianity and the often non-Christian Indigenous People he dealt with at Indian Affairs. Could the imagination be a tool for cultural amelioration? Could these very real tensions that threatened Canada be balanced creatively? Or would they destroy each other? Duncan Campbell Scott wrestled with his many contradictions in his poetry. In this way he tried to discover a solution through literature.

E. Pauline Johnson [Tekahionwake]

Poet of the Mohawk People

"To His Royal Highness The Duke of Connaught, Who is Head Chief of the Six Nations Indians, I inscribe this book by his own gracious permission" and "... both flint and feather bear the hall-mark of my Mohawk blood" seem at odds with each other. And yet, the first quote is the dedication of *Flint and Feather*[1] and the second quote closes her "Author's Foreword" in the same volume. Both are the words of E. Pauline Johnson.

E. (Emily) Pauline Johnson, whose Mohawk name was Tekahionwake, was the daughter of George H.M. Johnson, Head Chief of the Six Nations People, and Emily Howells, a British woman from Bristol, England. Johnson combined her roles of Mohawk Princess, as she often presented herself, and loyal subject of Queen Victoria with intelligence and grace. More importantly, Johnson spoke with the clearest voice for the Indigenous Peoples of her time. She was *both* a Mohawk and a Canadian patriot of the Confederation Period. And she was also a staunch supporter of what was known as Greater Britain, while in no way painting over the abuses Indigenous communities had suffered, and continued to suffer, at the hands of the English-speaking settlers. In fact, Johnson protested these abuses passionately.

In the past, critics commonly dismissed Johnson's work as lightweight, sentimental, and shallow, as if she were a sort of cut-rate Bliss Carman. She was also viewed as a sell-out who had been mainly interested in pleasing her non-Indigenous audiences. For example, Margaret Atwood's *The New Oxford Book of Canadian Verse in English*[2] offers its readers only two Johnson poems while including six each by Sir Charles G.D. Roberts and Archibald Lampman, five by Duncan Campbell Scott, and four by Wilfred Campbell. This assessment of Johnson as an inferior poet is now seen to have been false.[3] In fact, contemporary poets do read her poetry, and the present study will attempt to show why.

Pauline Johnson was born on the Six Nations Reserve near Brantford, Ontario on March 10, 1861. Sickly from early childhood, her life was not to be a long one. Her health began to fail while she was in her late forties, and she died at the age of fifty-two in Vancouver on March 7, 1913, the year following the publication of *Flint and Feather*. This book collects her poems from *The White Wampum*[4] and *Canadian Born*,[5] as well as twenty additional pieces. She also published stories in collections such as *Legends of Vancouver*,[6] *The Moccasin Maker*,[7] and *The Shagganappi*.[8] Although Johnson left the reserve near Brantford once her literary career was established, she was first and foremost a Mohawk woman, and she granted equal importance to both the Mohawk part and the female part of her identity.

Today, Johnson is read by anyone interested in the experience of a woman living in a male-dominated world, by anyone interested in the experience of an Indian (a term she habitually used to refer to herself) living in a White-dominated world, and by anyone interested in good poetry. Questions of politics, gender, and ethnicity aside, one can read her *Flint and Feather* for the enjoyment of well-made poetry. Like other poets of the Confederation Period, such as Archibald Lampman and Ethelwyn Wetherald, Johnson was an exceptional nature poet. One example of this is her poem about Lake Erie.[9]

Erie Waters

A dash of yellow sand,
Wind-scattered and sun-tanned;
Some waves that curl and cream along the margin of the strand;
And, creeping close to these
Long shores that lounge at ease,
Old Erie rocks and ripples to a fresh sou'western breeze.

A sky of blue and grey;
Some stormy clouds that play
At scurrying up with ragged edge, then laughing blow away,
Just leaving in their trail
Some snatches of a gale;
To whistling summer winds we lift a single daring sail.

O! wind so sweet and swift,
O! danger-freighted gift
Bestowed on Erie with her waves that foam and fall and lift,
We laugh in your wild face,
And break into a race
With flying clouds and tossing gulls that weave and interlace.

Marshes, both fresh water and, on the coasts, salt water, are common in Canada, and especially in the vast regions of Ontario and Québec covered by the Canadian Shield. Marshes abound with natural life of all sorts. They are of immense importance to our plant and animal ecosystems, and were of even greater importance to Indigenous people, who counted on them for food and fur like beaver, muskrats, waterfowl, rice, and other edible plants. Johnson was an outstanding poet of nature and "Marshlands"[10] shows her attention to detail.

Marshlands

A thin wet sky, that yellows at the rim,
And meets with sun-lost lip the marsh's brim.

The pools low lying, dank with moss and mould,
Glint through their mildews like large cups of gold.

Among the wild rice in the still lagoon,
In monotone the lizard shrills his tune.

The wild goose, homing, seeks a sheltering,
Where rushes grow, and oozing lichens cling.

Late cranes with heavy wing, and lazy flight,
Sail up the silence with the nearing night.

And like a spirit, swathed in some soft veil,
Steals twilight and its shadows o'er the swale.

Hushed lie the sedges, and the vapours creep,
Thick, grey and humid, while the marshes sleep.

Like other female writers of her period, such as Ethelwyn Wetherald and Isabella Valancy Crawford, Johnson never married. Perhaps it was only in the 20th century that a woman could have a career and also marry, so few seemed to be able to combine the two in one life. By contrast, almost all of the male writers of the Confederation Period married and fathered children. Whatever her reason for remaining single, Johnson's loneliness, her isolation, and her romantic longings form the subject of more than one poem. Another issue she faced was her mixed-race status. The poet was caught between two worlds. Because her mother was non-Native, Johnson was somewhat socially excluded by the matrilineal Mohawks. In the Mohawk world, an Indian had an Indian mother, and Johnson had an English mother. And White society was certainly not eager to welcome people who were half Indigenous in Victorian times.

Johnson dealt with the issue of mixed-race romance in her poem "The Pilot of the Plains."[11] In this poem, an Indigenous woman has a "Pale-face lover" and the members of her tribe try to discredit his love for her. They pressure her to marry her "Redskin wooer" who, they claim, is a "nobler warrior" than any White man could be. This is a tragic poem of two people bound together by true love because both the White lover and the Indigenous maiden die in a prairie blizzard. It is a good, well-made poem. And it suggests that the poet herself might have experienced a thwarted romance with a "Pale-faced" man, the barrier of racial prejudice being extremely difficult to overcome, both then and now.

An honest woman, Johnson also wrote about the brutal violence between different Indigenous Peoples. Her "As Red Men Die"[12] is a remarkable piece of writing for a Victorian woman in its unflinching investigation of this bitter subject. Clearly, there is nothing simple or one-sided about her understanding of complex issues. Johnson willingly takes up conflicts between different groups of Native people, conflicts between the Indigenous communities and their neighbouring settlers, the paternalistic relationship between the English and the far-flung pieces of Greater Britain, such as Canada, and the tensions that arise between men and women. To her credit, she refuses to opt for easy "black and white" solutions.

Although Britain had designated a large tract of land along both banks of the Grand River in Ontario to be a home for her Mohawk ancestors in recognition of their loyalty to the Crown in time of war, this land was being stolen by Canadian settlers until hardly any remains. (Indeed, disputes between the Six Nations and the government over this land grant continue to the present day.) Thus her great poem "The Corn Husker."[13]

The Corn Husker

Hard by the Indian lodges, where the bush
　　Breaks in a clearing, through ill-fashioned fields,
She comes to labour, when the first still hush
　　Of autumn follows large and recent yields.

Age in her fingers, hunger in her face,
　　Her shoulders stooped with weight of work and years,
But rich in tawny colouring of her race,
　　She comes a-field to strip the purple ears.

And all her thoughts are with the days gone by,
　　Ere might's injustice banished from their lands
Her people, that to-day unheeded lie,
　　Like the dead husks that rustle through her hands.

Johnson travelled across Canada and the United States many times, presenting readings to large audiences. From these coast-to-coast tours came poems celebrating our many regions: Halifax in the far east, her native and much beloved Ontario, Brandon, Manitoba, Saskatchewan's Qu'Appelle valley, Calgary, Alberta, Golden Mountain and British Columbia's Selkirk Mountains, and the Lost Lagoon of Vancouver's Stanley Park, where she is buried. The themes that supported both her life and her poetry are her Mohawk heritage, her Christianity, her love of Canada and its people, and her strong support for the British Crown and the Greater Britain of which Canada forms an important part. And central to her concerns is that Canada was loyal and did not side with the Americans in cutting the British connection. The initial two stanzas along with the closing stanza of "Canadian Born,"[14] will demonstrate my point:

Canadian Born

We first saw light in Canada, the land beloved of God;
We are the pulse of Canada, its marrow and its blood:
And we, the men of Canada, can face the world and brag
That we were born in Canada beneath the British flag.

Few of us have the blood of kings, few are of courtly birth,
But few are vagabonds or rogues of doubtful name and
worth;
And all have one credential that entitles us to brag—
That we were born in Canada beneath the British flag.

...

The Dutch may have their Holland, the Spaniard have his
Spain,
The Yankee to the south of us must south of us remain;
For not a man dare lift a hand against the men who brag
That they were born in Canada beneath the British flag.

This view that Canada should remain a strong—but independent—part of the British Empire was generally shared by the Canadian people, including many First Nations people of her time. (As a result of the unjust treaty process, Indigenous communities had good reason to place more trust in the Crown than in the newly established Canadian government, which displayed little interest in protecting their rights.) Johnson was no simple Canadian nationalist. She was proud to be a descendent of the literary tradition of Byron, Keats, and Tennyson, and she also cherished the poetry of Longfellow and a few of his fellow 19th century American poets. And still, Pauline Johnson always identified herself as a Mohawk woman. She intended to have the best of both worlds.

But it is her love for Ontario's landscapes that was perhaps her most constant support. When younger, Johnson enjoyed camping, and a few stanzas from her "Under Canvas"[15] will illustrate her love of nature:

Under Canvas

In Muskoka

Lichens of green and grey on every side;
And green and grey the rocks beneath our feet;
Above our heads the canvas stretching wide;
And over all, enchantment rare and sweet.

. . .

Across the lake the rugged islands lie,
Fir-crowned and grim; and further in the view
Some shadows seeming swung 'twixt cloud and sky,
Are countless shores, a symphony of blue.

. . .

The scent of burning leaves, the camp-fire's blaze,
The great logs cracking in the brilliant flame,
The groups grotesque, on which the firelight plays,
Are pictures which Muskoka twilights frame.

Johnson's most widely-read poem today, and one that has inspired generations of Canadian poets well into the 21st century, is "The Song My Paddle Sings"[16] from her first poetry collection, *The White Wampum*.

The Song My Paddle Sings

West wind, blow from your prairie nest
Blow from the mountains, blow from the west.
The sail is idle, the sailor too;
O! wind of the west, we wait for you.
Blow, blow!
I have wooed you so,
But never a favour you bestow.
You rock your cradle the hills between,
But scorn to notice my white lateen.

I stow the sail, unship the mast:
I wooed you long but my wooing's past;
My paddle will lull you into rest.
O! drowsy wind of the drowsy west,
Sleep, sleep,
By your mountain steep,
Or down where the prairie grasses sweep!
Now fold in slumber your laggard wings,
For soft is the song my paddle sings.

August is laughing across the sky,
Laughing while paddle, canoe and I,
Drift, drift,
Where the hills uplift
On either side of the current swift.

The river rolls in its rocky bed;
My paddle is plying its way ahead;
Dip, dip,
While the waters flip
In foam as over their breast we slip.

And oh, the river runs swifter now;
The eddies circle about my bow.
Swirl, swirl!
How the ripples curl
In many a dangerous pool awhirl!

And forward far the rapids roar,
Fretting their margin for evermore.
Dash, dash,
With a mighty crash,
They seethe, and boil, and bound, and splash.

Be strong, O paddle! be brave, canoe!
The reckless waves you must plunge into.
Reel, reel.
On your trembling keel,
But never a fear my craft will feel.

We've raced the rapid, we're far ahead!
The river slips through its silent bed.
Sway, sway,
As the bubbles spray
And fall in tinkling tunes away.

And up on the hills against the sky,
A fir tree rocking its lullaby,
Swings, swings,
Its emerald wings,
Swelling the song that my paddle sings.

It was not easy for a woman to have a successful literary career in her time, and even more so for an Indigenous woman. She achieved what she did through courage and determination. She never gave up. *Flint and Feather* closes with her death poem. In her final struggle with the forces of mortality, Johnson uses the metaphor of a real war. Defiant to the end, her poem ends with:

> They've shot my flag to ribbons, but in rents
> It floats above the height;
> Their ensign shall not crown my battlements
> While I can stand and fight.
> I fling defiance at them as I cry,
> "Capitulate? Not I."[17]

Ethelwyn Wetherald

Poet of the Eramosa

Among the most stunning regions of southern Ontario is the valley formed by the Eramosa River. This river flows from the village of Erin to the city of Guelph, on its way passing through Rockwood, a landscape rich in glacial potholes, rolling hills, and glorious scenery. Indeed, Rockwood is appropriately named because of its rocky escarpments, limestone outcroppings, and thick wooded areas. It was here, a decade before Confederation, that Agnes Ethelwyn Wetherald was born on April 26, 1857, one of eleven siblings. For a poet of grace and natural beauty, there was no better place to start her life.

Like many poets of her time, Wetherald's father was a clergyman, but in her case the Reverend William Wetherald was a Quaker, not an Anglican. Initially educated by her father, the founder of the Rockwood Academy, our young poet later attended the Friends' Boarding School in Union Springs, New York. She returned to Canada where she served as an editor at Toronto's *Globe* newspaper. A country girl at heart, city living failed to suit her. She spent much of her later life on a farm on Ontario's Niagara Peninsula, where she died on March 9, 1940.

Perhaps wishing to be independent in order to focus on her writing and editing, she never married. She did, however, at the age of fifty-four, adopt a child, Dorothy. Because it was most unusual for an unmarried woman to adopt a child in pre-World War I Canada, critics often consider Wetherald an early feminist. Whatever her reasons for remaining single, our poet wrote a series of children's verses for her young daughter that were collected and published as *Tree-Top Mornings.*[1]

Of her objection to sexism and the double standard there can be little doubt. Women in her day—and, sadly, our day too—were keenly aware of sexism in society. Wetherald was quick to note injustice, as her "Hester Prynne Speaks,"[2] a poem inspired by Nathaniel Hawthorne's novel *The Scarlet Letter*,[3] clearly shows.

Hester Prynne Speaks

Two fires are mine: one strong within, love-born;
One fierce without, of human hate and scorn,
And on my breast, my Pearl, my flower of fire.

Two woes are mine: the sharp pang of desire,
And that sick moan of her who anguished much
Until she found the Garment's hem to touch.

Two loves: my Pearl, and him who on my breast
Gave me my shame, my child, life's worst and best,
Of lowest hell, of highest heaven are such.

Two souls have I: one in these baby eyes,
One answering human scorn with scornful cries.
Lord, would I had Thy Garment's hem to touch!

Wetherald quickly developed into one of the leading nature poets in all of North America, with three of her six books being published in Boston. Critics compared her descriptive verse to the work of Archibald Lampman, Duncan Campbell Scott, and Bliss Carman. Wetherald was especially known for her poems about birds. Typical of her shorter lyrics is:

The Screech-Owl

Hearing the strange night-piercing sound
  Of woe that strove to sing,
I followed where it hid, and found
  A small soft-throated thing,
A feathered handful of gray grief,
Perched by the year's last leaf.

And heeding not that in the sky
  The lamps of peace were lit,
It sent abroad that sobbing cry,
  And sad hearts echoed it.
O hush, poor grief, so gray, so wild,
God still is with His child![4]

The current Poet of Rockwood, if I may use that term, is Katherine L. Gordon. In her unpublished piece "An Appreciation for Agnes Ethelwyn Wetherald,"[5] Gordon states:

> I live close to the birthplace of this exceptional, nature-attuned poet, have visited her home and childhood haunts. I knew at once where her spirit resided as I live now in a secluded tree-halloed river valley bordering on the Eramosa River that Ethelwyn would recognize. I know the birds that stirred her heart with their 'tender-throated' calls. I know the leaves that inform and colour my world, the loss of bird and spiralling leaves when winter stifles. Ethelwyn wrote of them with a seasonal sense of loss as I often do, her thoughts perhaps drifting down to me.

Despite much early success—Wetherald published her first poem in an American magazine when she was just seventeen and her initial collection, *The House of the Trees and Other Poems*, appeared as early as 1895—her poetry is almost unknown today. It was not always so. When her *The Last Robin: Lyrics and Sonnets* appeared in 1907, Earl Grey, then Governor General of Canada, purchased twenty-five copies of its first edition to give to his friends. And major Confederation Poets such as Archibald Lampman, Sir Charles G.D. Roberts, and Wilfred Campbell praised her poetry.[6]

In common with Canadian poets of every period, Wetherald wrote excellent winter poems:

A Winter Picture

An air as sharp as steel, a sky
    Pierced with a million points of fire;
The level fields, hard, white and dry,
    A road as straight and tense as wire.

No hint of human voice or face
    In frost below or fire above,
Save where the smoke's blue billowing grace
    Flies flag-like from the roofs of love.[7]

Every resident of rural Ontario can identify with her lines: "The level fields, hard, white and dry,/ A road as straight and tense as wire." And who has never marvelled at "smoke's blue billowing grace" on a frosty night?

February is very much winter in most of Ontario, all of Québec and Atlantic Canada, and on the prairies. Spring is nowhere in sight. But on the Niagara Peninsula, where Wetherald spent much of her life, people know that when February comes, spring must be just around the corner. In "To February,"[8] the poet warns winter that its days are numbered.

To February

O master-builder, blustering as you go
  About your giant work, transforming all
  The empty woods into a glittering hall,
And making lilac lanes and footpaths grow
As hard as iron under stubborn snow,
  Though every fence stand forth a marble wall,
  And windy hollows drift to arches tall,
There comes a might that shall your might o'erthrow.

Build high your white and dazzling palaces,
  Strengthen your bridges, fortify your towers,
    Storm with a loud and a portentous lip;
And April with a fragmentary breeze,
  And half a score of gentle, golden hours,
    Shall leave no trace of your stern workmanship.

One thing that sets her poetry apart from much of the nature poetry of the post-Confederation years is an erotic edge. The opening stanza of "Moonlight"[9] displays this:

When I see the ghost of night
  Stealing through my window-pane,
Silken sleep and silver light
  Struggle for my soul in vain;
Silken sleep all balmily
  Breathes upon my lids oppressed,
Till I sudden start and see
  Ghostly fingers on my breast.

Seeing the erotic potential in nature was also an important achievement of Isabella Valancy Crawford. While it is not known if Crawford and Wetherald knew each other personally, Wetherald wrote a perceptive 15-page introduction to Crawford's *Collected Poems*[10] in 1905.

Wetherald did address other topics; she was not solely a poet of the natural world. In *The Last Robin* she has poems that deal with growing old:

> But now the glowing book of life
>   Is falling from his nerveless hand;
> Gone are the splendors of the strife,
>   The conquering hopes—a daring band;[11]

Nonetheless, today her reputation rests on her nature poetry, as do the reputations of so many of her colleagues. As Gordon notes in her above-cited "Appreciation"—

> Her words are a vibrant music in the woods, lessons of nature, connections to the immortal spirit in all things. They can fill you still with truth and comfort. They above all deeply understand the human condition, and thus help to relieve it. She experienced much more than most Victorian women ever got to taste, she gleaned what we most appreciate of her journey, a lasting connection to our history of poetic achievement and message.

Helena Coleman

Poet of the First World War

While Helena Coleman is best known for her poetry of the First World War, she was also a noted poet of the natural world. Like so many of the other Confederation Poets, she was the child of a minister, in her case the Reverend Francis Coleman, a Methodist. The poet was born in Newcastle, Ontario on April 27, 1860, and attended the Ontario Ladies' College in nearby Whitby. She lived in Ontario her entire life. Like Susan Frances Harrison and other women of the period, Coleman tended to resort to a *nom de plume*, of which she used more than twenty.

In their "Afterword" to *Canadian Poetry: From the Beginnings Through the First World War*, Carole Gerson and Gwendolyn Davies note a "growing cultural nationalism" at the time of Confederation. This is to be found in all of the major poets who dominated the period: Isabella Valancy Crawford, Wilfred Campbell, Sir Charles G.D. Roberts, Bliss Carman, Archibald Lampman, and Duncan Campbell Scott. And in this context, Gerson and Davies also list two more women, Agnes Ethelwyn Wetherald and Pauline Johnson. What made these poets especially Canadian was their sense of Canadian geography, of our seasons, and they embodied a feeling for Canada's social history. These poets were able to express the Canadian experience in a manner their readers could readily identify with and understand. That is, rather than attempt to write like Victorian Englishmen touring the Lake District, they were writing about Canada for other Canadians. They worked to discover what made Canada different from other nations. And for the writers of their period, this difference started with Canada's landscape and seasons. Their poetry was intended to be a poetry of place: *this* place.

While the above holds true of Helena Coleman, what sets her apart from her colleagues is that she did not bring out a poetry collection until the 20th century. She was the last of her generation to break into print, and her *Songs and Sonnets* was published in 1906 by the Tennyson Club, when she was well into middle age. Coleman's best-known book, however, appeared eleven years later. Her *Marching Men: War Verses* was issued in 1917, during the Great War. Even though this war affected all who lived through it, more than most poets of her generation, Coleman's poetic vision was marked by the suffering war inflicted on both Europe and Canada.

It is, however, as a nature poet that she helped shape Canada by creating lasting images of our various landscapes. A good example of Helena Coleman's poetry of place is "On the Trail."[1] In this piece, Coleman finds herself on the great prairie with a storm brewing. Here are some stanzas that give the flavour of her verse:

On the Trail

Oh, there's nothing like the prairie
  When the wind is in your face,
And a thunder-storm is brewing,
  And night comes down apace—
'Tis then you feel the wonder
  And immensity of space!

Far in the gathering darkness
  Against the dying day
The ghostly hills are lying,
  The hills that stand for aye—
How in the dusk they glimmer
  And palpitate away!

…

How vast the world and void!
  No living thing in sight,
As to the lonely prairie
  Comes down the lonely night,
But in your heart what freedom—
  What sense of buoyant flight!

Once more the pulses quicken
  With life's exultant pride,
With hope and high ambition,
  As on and on you ride,
Till all the old desires
  Come galloping beside!

Oh, there's nothing like the prairie
  When the wind is in your face,
And the boom of distant thunder
  Comes rolling up apace—
'Tis then you feel the wonder
  And immensity of space!

Any reader familiar with the Canadian prairies will see at once how her poem is true to nature.

The seasons of Canada are a frequent topic, especially winter. It is difficult to think of a Canadian poet without several winter poems to his or her credit. It is also true that most, if not all, Confederation Poets have a poem called "Indian Summer." Here is Coleman's:[2]

Indian Summer

Of all Earth's varied, lovely moods,
The loveliest is when she broods
Among her dreaming solitudes
  On Indian Summer days;

When on the hill the aster pales,
And Summer's stress of passion fails,
And Autumn looks through misty veils
    Along her leafy ways.

How deep the tenderness that yearns
Within the silent wood that turns
From green to gold, and slowly burns
    As by some inward fire!
How dear the sense that all things wild
Have been at last by love beguiled
To join one chorus, reconciled
    In satisfied desire!

The changing hillside, wrapped in dreams,
With softest opalescent gleams,
Like some ethereal vision seems,
    Outlined against the sky;
The fields that gave the harvest gold—
Afar before our eyes unrolled
In purple distance, fold on fold—
    Lovely and tranquil lie.

We linger by the crimson vine,
Steeped to the heart with fragrant wine,
And where the rowan-berries shine,
    And gentians lift their blue;
We stay to hear the wind that grieves
Among the oak's crisp, russet leaves,
And watch the moving light, that weaves
    Quaint patterns, peering through.

The fires that in the maples glow,
The rapture that the beeches know,
The smoke-wraiths drifting to and fro,
  Each season more endears;
Vague longings in the heart arise,
A dimming mist comes to the eyes
That is not sadness, though it lies
  Close to the place of tears.

We share the ecstasy profound
That broods in everything around,
And by the wilderness are crowned—
  Its silent worship know.
O when our Indian Summer days
Divide the parting of the ways,
May we, too, linger here in praise
  Awhile before we go!

Although Coleman did not publish her first collection until six years into the 20th century, her "Indian Summer" reads very much like a 19th century poem, especially with the Romantic stance the poet adopts as she explores her subject. The reader will think of the nature odes of Keats, although without his flourishes and classical allusions. This shows how Helena Coleman could take a British model and make it Canadian in tone.

Coleman often published in leading American periodicals such as the *Atlantic Monthly*, as was the case with many other Confederation Poets. The simple fact was that most of the quality literary periodicals of her time were American, not Canadian.

While many of the Confederation Poets were happy to stay at home, a few—Sir Charles G.D. Roberts, Sophia M. Almon Hensley, Bliss Carman—had the urge to travel. Helena Coleman was among their number, as "Among the Mountains"[3] shows.

Among the Mountains

As far as sight could reach the wild peaks rose,
    Tier after tier against the limpid blue,
    Titanic forms that stormed the heavens anew
At every turn, crowned with imperial snows;
And then, as day sank softly to its close,
    Diaphanous, ethereal they grew,
    Mere wraiths of rainbow-mist that from our view,
Dream-laden, lapsed to darkness and repose.

And suddenly I found my vision blurred,
    And knew that deeper chord was touched again
Which once in Hungary, when I had heard
    A passionately wild, appealing strain
Of gypsy music, left me strangely stirred
    With incommunicable joy and pain.

As noted in the chapter on Susan Frances Harrison, it was often women who took up the topic of aging and lost youth. (Male poets seldom addressed this issue.) Coleman had this to say:

Vanished Years

She sitteth in the sunshine, old and gray,
    Her faded kerchief crossed upon her breast,
    Her withered form in sober colors dressed,
Her eyes deep-sunken in far memory;
She scarcely sees the children at their play,
    But looks beyond them to the crimsoning west—
    And still beyond, where everlasting rest
Remains to close and crown her little day.

But on her tranquil and unconscious face,
  In lines engraved by joy no less than tears,
The story of her pilgrimage we trace,
    For Youth, quick-flying, left his dearer part,
  And all the fragrance of the vanished years,
    Imperishable, lies within her heart.[4]

As a woman, Coleman watched the First World War from afar. This conflict was so devastating that just about every Canadian family felt its impact. Among the poems in her 1917 collection is:

When First He Put the Khaki On

When first he put the khaki on
  He tried with careful art
To seem blasé and casual
  And play the proper part,
But it was plain as plain could be
  He was a child at heart.

Although he talked in knowing terms
  Of what "the boys" had done,
Likewise of ammunition tests,
  And how to load a gun,
And bragged that in his stocking feet
  He stood full six foot, one.

Yet all the while the child looked out
  With mild appealing eyes,
Unconscious he was visible
  Beneath the man's disguise,
Nor dreaming what the look evoked
  In hearts grown mother-wise.

How could he know the sudden pang,
  The stir of swift alarms,
The yearning prayer that innocence
  Be kept from all the harms,
The inner reach of tenderness,
  And cradling of soft arms?[5]

Coleman's final publication was *Songs*[6] in 1937, a modest selection of her earlier work. She did not publish during the last quarter-century of her life.[7] Perhaps her poetry could no longer fit into the Canada of post-war sensibilities. Helena Coleman lived until December 7, 1953 (the same year Elvis Presley recorded "That's When Your Heartaches Begin" at Sun Records). In many respects she remained the poet of the First World War, and the "new" Canada of the 1950s was a world a poet like Helena Coleman would not have liked.

Conclusion

The story of our Confederation Poets began in Dublin, Ireland on Christmas Day, 1850 when Isabella Valancy Crawford was born. It closed over a century later on August 3, 1954 with the death in Montréal of William Douw Lighthall.[1] By the time they were done, our writers had established a Canadian literature and defined a Canadian culture. They pointed out a path their new nation might follow into the 20th century. And they inspired an entire generation of 20th century writers like Dorothy Livesay, Al Purdy, Milton Acorn, and Raymond Souster. A couple of the Confederation Poets actually formed a bridge to the next generation. Livesay published *Green Pitcher* in 1928; Purdy published *The Enchanted Echo* in 1944; Souster and Irving Layton published, respectively, *When We Are Young* and *Here and Now* in 1945. Confederation Poet Duncan Campbell Scott published his last book in 1947.

A few of these men and women—Archibald Lampman, Isabella Valancy Crawford, Sir Charles G.D. Roberts, and E. Pauline Johnson —left a large handprint on our literature. Others—George Frederick Cameron, Helena Coleman, and Sophia M. Almon Hensley—made a more modest mark. Nonetheless, each and every one contributed importantly to the Canada we have today. In general, the Confederation writers, of both poetry and fiction, came from the middle or professional class. Their fathers were often ministers, doctors, lawyers, or teachers, and the writers usually enjoyed a university education. Despite the success of poets like Charles Sangster, writers coming from a working class background did not become common until after the First World War. While Isabella Valancy Crawford died in poverty, and Pauline Johnson ended her days being supported by the charity of her friends, most of these writers lived middle-class lives. This set them apart from the general population.

Like Sir John A. Macdonald, the writers of the Confederation Period tended to be politically conservative and Canadian federalists in that they supported a united country as opposed to a more loosely-knit confederation of provinces. They, as noted throughout this study, supported a united Canada *within* the British Empire. They cherished their British traditions. Queen Victoria was generally admired by members of all social and educational classes in Canada. People were quite wary of American expansionism, which they considered to represent a threat to Canada. With rare exceptions, like Bliss Carman, they distrusted the United States and its culture, and they rejected the American model of complete independence.

It is well worth recalling that when Canada started in 1867, our nation was to be bilingual French and English, bi-religious Roman Catholic and Protestant, and bi-political Conservative and Liberal.[2] Our linguistic, religious, and political differences, strong as they might grow from time to time, would be put in the background so as to engender a united country. Not only was our bilingualism/biculturalism necessary to produce a united Canadian federation, along with our connection to Britain and the Crown, it also marked us as different from the Americans to the south, the great melting pot. The crucial nature of this was reaffirmed almost a hundred years later when, in 1963, Prime Minister Lester B. Pearson established The Royal Commission on Bilingualism and Biculturalism/Commission royale d'enquête sur le bilinguisme et le biculturalisme, also called the Bi and Bi Commission. And it was reaffirmed yet again almost twenty years after that with Prime Minister Pierre Elliott Trudeau's Constitution Act of 1982.

Nearly all of our Confederation Poets had strong connections to the landscape of either the Canadian/Laurentian Shield in Ontario and Québec or the Appalachian system in the Maritimes. The major cultural and academic centres of the Confederation Period were Halifax, Fredericton, Montréal, Ottawa, and Kingston. These were the host cities of Dalhousie University, the University of New

Brunswick, McGill University, the University of Ottawa, and Queen's University, the young nation's leading centres of learning.

Our important poets connected to Nova Scotia and New Brunswick were George Frederick Cameron, Bliss Carman, Barry Straton, Sophia M. Almon Hensley, John Frederic Herbin, and Sir Charles G.D. Roberts. Our poets with connections to Montréal and Québec City were Susan Frances Harrison (although she spent her life in Toronto), William Douw Lighthall, and Frederick George Scott. Our leading poets associated with Ottawa were Wilfred Campbell, Archibald Lampman, and Duncan Campbell Scott. And connected to the western Shield region of Ontario during her formative years was Isabella Valancy Crawford (Paisley and Peterborough).

Only three of our poets had no meaningful connection to the landscapes of the Canadian Shield/Appalachian System: Helena Coleman, E. Pauline Johnson, and Ethelwyn Wetherald. And although both Crawford and Harrison would live and work in Toronto and maintain an association with that city, the only poet completely and deeply rooted to the Toronto area (Whitby) was Coleman.

I do not believe that we can risk overlooking the significance of the above facts. Halifax, Fredericton, Montréal, Ottawa, Kingston and the hinterland surrounding them, such as the Bay of Fundy, the Laurentians, and the Gatineaus, formed the old, or *original*, geography of French and English Canada. (To the west of Kingston lay the much "newer" Canada of places to be settled later.) While our country has greatly expanded beyond its Halifax-to-Kingston foundation, the roots of English-language culture are to be found there and our culture will remain strong and Canadian as long as these roots are nurtured.

All of our English-language writers began life as Christians, and many were Anglican even if, later in life, they questioned some of their church's dogma. They were men and women of their time, and shared the strengths and prejudices of the middle class of their period. But they were also visionaries. They understood that the creation of a Canadian literature was the work set before them by circumstance. Their new nation required a culture and this they would provide.

While they were inspired by British and, to a lesser degree, American literary models, they did not attempt to be little Wordsworths or little Longfellows. (Imitation only works for the young as part of their learning process.) They sought to write as Canadians for Canadians. To do so they knew they had to develop a Canadian idiom for their new land.

This is not to suggest that readers will not find echoes of Keats in Archibald Lampman, echoes of Longfellow in Pauline Johnson, or echoes of Wordsworth in Wilfred Campbell. And sometimes it is possible to discern more than mere echoes. But our Confederation Poets tried to keep these to a minimum. They may have been proud heirs of the grandeur of English literature, but they did not wish to be mere slaves to tradition. In their mature writings they succeeded more often than they failed.

To get the ball rolling, Sir Charles G.D. Roberts published *Orion, and Other Poems* in 1880. That was over a hundred and forty years ago, and a great deal has changed. For one thing, the general unity of vision present during the 1880s and 1890s has fragmented into many views of Canada. In 1880, Canada was composed of three cultural regions: the Maritimes, Québec, and Ontario. Today there are many more regions and sub-regions. In 1880, most people were religious and attended a church, often an Anglican or Roman Catholic house of worship. There were hardly any Jews in the country and Muslims were unknown. Today there are several religious communities, including Hindus and Buddhists. And many, if not most, Canadians are not religious at all. In 1880, most people lived on farms, in villages, or in small towns. Their economy was largely agrarian. Today's Canada is urban and most Canadians live in or near one of the nation's dozen major cities. Also new today, Indigenous Canadians have in recent years stepped forward in the arts and literature, and this must be taken into account by all commentators on our national culture. (For too long that was not true, and these First Canadians were ignored.) Terms like the "Canadian people" and "Canadian culture" have become difficult to quantify. Questions like "Who are the Canadian people?" and "What is our culture like?" are often asked in academic and political circles. In some quarters, "cultural values" have become a crucial point of heated debate. (In 2018 a group of writers, largely Toronto-based, went so far as to claim that Canadians no longer existed *as a people* because the people here have too little in common.)

One might ask: "What can the Confederation Poets teach 21st century Canadians?" A lot, in fact, as we have seen. To fully understand where we are, we need to appreciate where we started. Their vision of an English-speaking nation with strong British roots composed of committed Christians no longer holds true. But then, neither England nor the United States is today what it was a century and a half ago. All change is not for the worse. Some change is welcome and benefits humanity. Few today would enjoy living like their great-grandparents. Nonetheless, there is much that was true and honourable and valuable in the Confederation Period that has been lost to society today. As Winston Churchill wisely observed, a nation that forgets its past has no future. Fortunately, reading the Confederation Poets might help return to us The True North they recognized. The True North is, after all, still there.

Epilogue

Confederation Poetry in the Postmodern Era

Canadian poetry in English, as Canadian poetry, started in the pre-Modern 19th century, a time of political conservatism and almost universal religious observation, a time of the high Romanticism of Keats and Shelley and the Victorianism of Tennyson and Arnold in the literary arts. Our poetry continued throughout the era of Modernism, signalled by the carnage of World War I. And it finds itself over a century and a half later in the midst of literary Postmodernism and a post-Modern world. Needless to say, much has changed. The Red Tories may be gone, but those old roots remain. Many poets today still read the Confederation Poets.

Just as the generation of the Confederation Poets came to an end with the death of William Douw Lighthall on August 3, 1954, so the Great Generation Poets they directly influenced and inspired ended on July 12, 2017 when Simcha (Sam) Simchovitch died in Toronto. But this in no way means that the Confederation Poets have been relegated to dusty and ignored library shelves.

During the coronavirus plague of the spring of 2020, I wrote to fifty contemporary poets to see what, if anything, the Confederation Poets meant to them and their poetry. Thirty-one poets responded from Charlottetown, Prince Edward Island and Moncton, New Brunswick in the east to Vancouver and Victoria, British Columbia in the west. Not only have contemporary poets been influenced by the poetry of the 1880s and 1890s via the works of the Great Generation Poets they knew personally, they have also been *directly* influenced by their 19th century predecessors by reading their poems. In fact, some contemporary poets were initially inspired to write poetry by poets like Lampman, Campbell, and Johnson.

Although it is unfortunately true that many of the poets studied here are hardly known today, Bliss Carman, Pauline Johnson, Archibald Lampman, Wilfred Campbell, and Sir Charles G.D. Roberts are being read and enjoyed two decades into the 21st century. Even though their books may be long out-of-print, facsimile editions of their early collections are quite often available.

By far the most popular of our Confederation Poets is Archibald Lampman. As noted in the chapter on Lampman, he was poised on the cusp of Modernism. In a real sense, our poet indicated a bridge from the Victorian poetry all of our poets were writing when they were starting out to the poetry that was to come following the First World War. (Lampman, it should be noted, died while Queen Victoria was still on the throne.) To clearly display the difference, here are two poems with the same title. In Lampman's initial poetry collection we find "In November"[1] which is a sonnet in the style of the Victorian verse of his day.

In November

The hills and leafless forests slowly yield
  To the thick-driving snow. A little while
  And night shall darken down. In shouting file
The woodmen's carts go by me homeward-wheeled,
Past the thin fading stubbles, half concealed,
  Now golden-grey, sowed softly through with snow,
  Where the last ploughman follows still his row,
Turning black furrows through the whitening field.

Far off the village lamps begin to gleam,
  Fast drives the snow, and no man comes this way;
    The hills grow wintry white, and bleak winds moan
    About the naked uplands. I alone
  Am neither sad, nor shelterless, nor grey,
Wrapped round with thought, content to watch and dream.

This poem was published in 1888. It deals with a common topic for Canadian poets: the onset of winter. It also displays Lampman's skill with the sonnet. As such, it is a fine, well-made poem for the 1880s.

Seven years later, in 1895, Lampman published a second "In November"[2] in his second collection.

In November

With loitering step and quiet eye,
Beneath the low November sky,
I wandered in the woods, and found
A clearing, where the broken ground
Was scattered with black stumps and briers,
And the old wreck of forest fires.
It was a bleak and sandy spot,
And, all about, the vacant plot
Was peopled and inhabited
By scores of mulleins long since dead.
A silent and forsaken brood
In that mute opening of the wood,
So shrivelled and so thin they were,
So gray, so haggard, and austere,
Not plants at all they seemed to me,
But rather some spare company
Of hermit folk, who long ago,
Wandering in bodies to and fro,
Had chanced upon this lonely way,
And rested thus, till death one day
Surprised them at their compline prayer,
And left them standing lifeless there.

There was no sound about the wood
Save the wind's secret stir. I stood
Among the mullein-stalks as still

As if myself had grown to be
One of their sombre company,
A body without wish or will.
And as I stood, quite suddenly,
Down from a furrow in the sky
The sun shone out a little space
Across that silent sober place,
Over the sand heaps and brown sod,
The mulleins and dead goldenrod,
And passed beyond the thickets gray,
And lit the fallen leaves that lay,
Level and deep within the wood,
A rustling yellow multitude.

And all around me the thin light,
So sere, so melancholy bright,
Fell like the half-reflected gleam
Or shadow of some former dream;
A moment's golden reverie
Poured out on every plant and tree
A semblance of weird joy, or less,
A sort of spectral happiness;
And I, too, standing idly there,
With muffled hands in the chill air,
Felt the warm glow about my feet,
And shuddering betwixt cold and heat,
Drew my thoughts closer, like a cloak,
While something in my blood awoke,
A nameless and unnatural cheer,
A pleasure secret and austere.

These two poems are considered to be so important that both Raymond Souster in *Comfort of the Fields* and Carole Gerson and Gwendolyn Davies in their *Canadian Poetry: From the Beginnings*

Through the First World War include both versions to show the development of Lampman's prosody and approach to poetry. Indeed, Bruce Meyer ranks the 1895 "In November" as "the first modern Canadian poem."[3] The change in what Lampman thought poetry should be over seven short years is striking. This is a development even more noticeable in Lampman's third book, *Alcyone*.[4]

The 1888 sonnet concludes with the poet protected by his thoughts and starting to dream: "Wrapped round with thought, content to watch and dream." And the 1895 poem in rhymed couplets references a "shadow of some former dream" and again the poet is protected from the reality of winter and death by drawing his "thoughts closer, like a cloak." The sonnet is a proper Victorian poem in all respects. It is somewhat romantic and soft rather than hard. But the later version displays a more contemporary sensitivity and, in a real sense, can be said to truly anticipate Modernism.

George Bowering cites "We Too Shall Sleep"[5] as an affective poem that escapes from the world of late Romantic English verse. It deals with the death of Lampman's young son, Archibald Otto, and was published in his third collection, the final one the poet assembled during his brief life. He died while it was in press, never seeing his book in print.

We Too Shall Sleep

Not, not for thee,
Beloved child, the burning grasp of life
Shall bruise the tender soil. The noise, and strife,
And clamour of midday thou shalt never see,
But wrapt for ever in thy quiet grave,
Too little to have known the earthly lot,
Time's clashing hosts above thine innocent head,
Wave upon wave,
Shall break, or pass as with an army's tread,
And harm thee not.

A few short years
We of the living flesh and restless brain
Shall plumb the deeps of life and know the strain,
The fleeting gleams of joy, the fruitless tears,
And then at last when all is touched and tried,
Our own immutable night shall fall, and deep
In the same silent plot, O little friend,
Side by thy side,
In peace that changeth not, nor knoweth end,
We too shall sleep.

In fact, the only poem Bowering mentions by name in commenting on Canada's Confederation Poets is Lampman's "We Too Shall Sleep."[6] (He mentions William Wilfred Campbell by name, and then passes on.) Except for the use of words like "thine" and "changeth," this poem reads like a modern, not a Victorian, poem. It certainly sounds 20th century, and that cannot be said of other Canadian poets of the 1890s. At the time of his death in 1899, "The City of the End of Things" and "We Too Shall Sleep" show a poet leading the way into modern verse.

For his part, Allan Briesmaster was so inspired by Lampman's poetry that he has published two homages: "Summer Twilight" (after Lampman's "A Summer Evening") and "Winter Night, Looking North" (after "Winter Solitude").[7] Another poet influenced by Lampman is A.F. Moritz, who writes: "I loved Lampman's 'The City of the End of Things' and it is very clearly present in the many last-man and ruined-future poems I have written ..."[8]

Lampman was born in Morpeth, Kent County, in Southwestern Ontario. It is perhaps to be expected that two poets closely associated with that region—John B. Lee and Keith Inman—have long been affected by Lampman's poetry. John B. Lee hails from Highgate, Ontario, quite near Morpeth, where his own great-grandfather was the village blacksmith.[9] In Lee's opinion, "The field of hay in Lampman's poem 'Heat' seems very much more likely to be a hay field in Kent than in the Ottawa valley." This view is shared by Keith Inman in his "I Sometimes Stop By Archie's Place"[10] which starts with: "Lampman's 'Heat' was one of the most inspirational poems I ever read when I started learning poetry. [T]he poem just stays with me, as does Lampman, who keeps crossing my path like a signpost."

Our Parliamentary Poet Laureate, George Elliott Clarke, makes an important point. Clarke writes: "[O]f interest to me, as a poet whose treatment of nature was vital, is Archie Lampman. He was perhaps the first English-Canadian poet to write comfortably of the non-British realities of Canadian Nature, to recognize that our winters are crisp, long, deep, dark, and potentially deadly ..."[11] While most of the Confederation Poets attempted to write as Canadians for Canadians, Lampman was the first who enjoyed genuine success in this endeavour. But Lampman's influence goes beyond his fellow writers and the literary community. By pointing out the raw, natural beauty of Canada, Lampman directed attention to something that set Canada apart from England. Clarke goes on to add: "In a sense, he was the poet who led the way to the Group of Seven." (An opinion I share with Professor Clarke.)

Finally, Colin Morton, a poet based in Ottawa and a recipient of the Archibald Lampman Award, notes that "Interest in Lampman and his contemporaries has been steady in Ottawa. I was involved with the Ottawa Literary Heritage group, started by Steve Artelle ... His Beechwood Cemetery tours and other events kept alive memories of the little cultural capital that tentatively developed in Ottawa after Confederation."[12] Far from being forgotten, a hundred and forty-two years following the publication of Sir Charles G.D. Roberts' first book, Confederation poetry still lives.

The second most widely read poet by contemporary writers is E. Pauline Johnson. Given how many people are reading and studying Johnson's poetry today, it seems remarkable that Jack David and Robert Lecker chose not to include her in their two-volume anthology, *Canadian Poetry.* (Fortunately, Johnson's poetry has been properly represented by Carole Gerson and Gwendolyn Davies in their *Canadian Poetry: From the Beginnings Through the First World War.*)

Johnson, as noted in her chapter, was a Mohawk woman from the Six Nations First Nation in Ontario. She often used her Mohawk name, Tekahionwake, and she is the only Indigenous poet of her time popular today. In fact, she is the only non-White Confederation Poet read today. Johnson came from a period when published writers were for the most part both White and male. Confederation women, even extremely fine writers like Isabella Valancy Crawford, struggled to get their books published and read. Women were simply not taken seriously. They were expected to become wives and mothers, not writers or artists. Thus, Pauline Johnson becomes a heroic figure in Canadian literature. Her courage and the lyric power of her verse continue to inspire poets today.

Tom Wayman writes that the two most important Confederation Poets for him have been Wilfred Campbell and E. Pauline Johnson. The rhyme and metre of Johnson's "The Song My Paddle Sings" made him "conscious of the oral nature of poetry. Even though my poems are written in free verse, they are meant to exist on the page as scores for oral delivery—all of my poems are worked and reworked in the process of composition until they sound satisfactory to me in the ear."[13] Indeed, all contemporary poets who cite Johnson as an inspiration list "The Song My Paddle Sings" as a work that has left a lasting impression.

Afro-Métis writer George Elliott Clarke cites Johnson "as a symbol of Indigenous/racialized accomplishment ... a figure whose poetics I needed to study."[14] Likewise, Saskatchewan's Marion Mutala, who identifies as Ukrainian-Canadian, views Johnson as a fellow writer whose "work blends two cultures."[15] Mutala adds, "As a contemporary writer, I can identity with her struggles, love of Canada and her heritage, though sometimes conflicting. Johnson, a key figure in the construction of Canadian literature has made her mark on Indigenous women's writing but also has opened the roads for others."

For Elana Wolff, it was Johnson's poetry that taught her of "the energized 'inner voice' I'd found by accident in 'The Song My Paddle Sings,' which showed me what could be achieved through poems."[16]

Wolff's own poetry seeks to release this "inner voice." Karen Shenfeld was also impressed by "The Song My Paddle Sings." Shenfeld notes the influence the poems of Archibald Lampman and Pauline Johnson had on her own work while she was writing the poems in her collection *My Father's Hands Spoke in Yiddish.* In Johnson's case, Shenfeld, a Jewish-Canadian poet, was "intrigued to discover a cycle of quiet, subtle poems that she wrote inspired by her Christian faith that were strikingly different from the poems that had made her famous."[17] More than a century after Johnson wrote her poem, it showed Shenfeld an approach to poetry she wanted to adapt and use in her own work.

While Johnson might be the only 19th century Indigenous poet read for pleasure today, she was not the first to break into print and develop a following. Before her was Ojibwa writer Kah-Ge-Ga-Gah-Bowh (or George Copway, as he is often known today). Born four years prior to Charles Sangster in 1818, he lived to see Confederation and died in 1869. His *The Life, History, and Travels of Kah-Ge-Ga-Gah-Bowh* was published in the United States (Albany, New York: Weed and Parsons, 1847). Although mostly prose, it contains some poetry and is available as a digital download from the University of Georgia. While quite popular during his lifetime—much like Johnson, he toured the U.S. and enjoyed a large public—Kah-Ge-Ga-Gah-Bowh soon fell from view. Today only scholars study his writings.

Perhaps the most widely read and most widely loved of all of the poems written during the Confederation Period is Wilfred Campbell's "Indian Summer." Of this poem Tom Wayman has written:

> Campbell's poem evokes the Eastern Canadian woods in fall.
>
> Along the line of smoky hills
> The crimson forest stands,
> And all the day the blue-jay calls
> Throughout the autumn lands.

> The setting is an expanse of maple and sumac whose leaves have turned, as the poem describes, on a 'long, still autumn day'. The poem exactly matches a memory of walking as a child with my parents on a trail or road through a woodland like that, with the trees flaming golden and red around us in the deep quiet of a windless fall afternoon.[18]

"Indian Summer" played a role in the young Becky D. Alexander becoming a poet. As a Grade 5 student she was asked to memorize a poem. Decades later Alexander notes:

> I remember becoming fascinated with Campbell's Indian Summer and I kept practising at it until it was fully memorized. It was the first poem that truly caught my eye, as it is so amazingly visual, and remains my personal favourite, as it does for many Canadians: there is a reason why it is so beloved. I could always understand and 'jump right into' his poems.[19]

And for Ottawa-based writer Blaine Marchand this was to happen in Grade 7. He recalls:

> Unbeknown to me, a Confederation poet inspired me to write poetry. My grade seven teacher, Mrs. Davis, loved poetry and would recite it to us. For two or three years, I had kept a school notebook and filled its pages with stories about animals, all of which possessed human characteristics, and people struggling with right and wrong, most likely as a result of my Catholic schooling and my eleven-year-old imagination.
>
> I can still recall that autumn of 1960 when Mrs. Davis stood before us and in an enunciated voice that filled the classroom, she began—'Along the line of smoky

> hills/ The crimson forest stands,/ And all the day the blue-jay calls/ Throughout the autumn lands.'
>
> Our teacher, after each recitation, would talk about how imagery worked and how in reciting poetry your voice should reflect and infuse the words with its music and emotion. She had me hooked. I loved the flow of poetry's lines, the way words could paint scenes and convey how you felt. I began trying my hand at poetry, piecing words and images together like a jigsaw.
>
> In high school, Mr. McElligott, my English teacher, encouraged my interest in poetry. In that heady year of Canada's centennial, the interest in Canadian writers increased. Mr. McElligott ensured that the Canadian poets, particularly the work of Archibald Lampman, were poems we studied. Many of the Confederation Poets had lived in Ottawa. Their love of nature and the areas around the region appealed to me. They described a landscape with which I was familiar and which still existed at that time. Also, the idea of the poet as a contemplative wanderer, in tune with nature, was how I envisioned the role of a writer.[20]

West Coast writer Linda Rogers counts Bliss Carman as a cousin, so perhaps she had a "genetic predisposition" (as she put it) towards his "Low Tide on Grand Pré." And although Rogers has had many influences in the world of poetry since that early introduction to Carman's verse, as she says, "I am a rebel. I do not follow recipes or the prescriptions of the patriarchy. I follow my heart and that is, for me, a reliable metric, but I do remember Bliss Carman because he was always there."[21] And Carman's great poem has always been there in the background for generations of Canadian poets. Many people writing today clearly remember three poems from the Confederation Period: Johnson's "The Song My Paddle Sings," Wilfred Campbell's "Indian Summer," and Carman's "Low Tide on Grand Pré."[22]

Low Tide on Grand Pré

The sun goes down, and over all
    These barren reaches by the tide
Such unelusive glories fall,
    I almost dream they yet will bide
    Until the coming of the tide.

And yet I know that not for us,
    By any ecstasy of dream,
He lingers to keep luminous
    A little while the grievous stream,
    Which frets, uncomforted of dream—

A grievous stream, that to and fro
    Athrough the fields of Acadie
Goes wandering, as if to know
    Why one beloved face should be
    So long from home and Acadie.

Was it a year or lives ago
    We took the grasses in our hands,
And caught the summer flying low
    Over the waving meadow lands,
    And held it there between our hands?

The while the river at our feet—
    A drowsy inland meadow stream—
At set of sun the after-heat
    Made running gold, and in the gleam
    We freed our birch upon the stream.

There down along the elms at dusk
  We lifted dripping blade to drift,
Through twilight scented fine like musk,
  Where night and gloom awhile uplift,
  Nor sunder soul and soul adrift.

And that we took into our hands
  Spirit of life or subtler thing—
Breathed on us there, and loosed the bands
  Of death, and taught us, whispering,
  The secret of some wonder-thing.

Then all your face grew light, and seemed
  To hold the shadow of the sun;
The evening faltered, and I deemed
  That time was ripe, and years had done
  Their wheeling underneath the sun.

So all desire and all regret,
  And fear and memory, were naught;
One to remember or forget
  The keen delight our hands had caught;
  Morrow and yesterday were naught.

The night has fallen, and the tide . . . .
  Now and again comes drifting home,
Across these aching barrens wide,
  A sigh like driven wind or foam:
  In grief the flood is bursting home.

Although living near the Bay of Fundy-Tantramar region in Moncton, not too far from the area Carman described so vividly, Margaret Patricia Eaton was mostly attracted to Carman's Transcendentalism. In two letters to me, Eaton observed that, "I think many of my poems have some variation of Transcendentalism ..."[23] and "I think there is a transcendental link to some of Carman's work ..."[24] As to her own spiritual leanings, Eaton states, "I think some of my poems suggest that we find God through our own meditation and connection with nature and less through organized religion or the intermediary of a priest or pastor ... and I think that is Carman's view point as well ..."[25] This is a sentiment with which Bliss Carman could agree.

It's interesting that Margaret Patricia Eaton is related to the noted writer and historian Arthur Wentworth Hamilton Eaton (December 10, 1849–July 11, 1937) who, had he only been born three weeks later, could have been part of our story of the Confederation Poets. The elder Eaton was the author of *Acadian Legends and Lyrics*; *Acadian Ballads, and De Soto's Last Dream*; *Poems of the Christian Year*; and *The Lotus of the Nile and Other Poems*. He shared several aspects of the poets covered here, and is worth looking into today, especially since he took up the Acadians and that chapter of Canadian culture.

Two other 21st century poets were attracted to Carman's later poetry, especially his long, rambling foot journeys outlined in books such as *Songs From Vagabondia* (1894). Like many Canadian poets, Marty Gervais was introduced to the Confederation Poets at a young age: "I grew up with the poetry of Bliss Carman. I found his books in the Bracebridge Public Library when I was 12 or 13. ... I was fascinated with 'The Joys of the Open Road' which contained his famous 'Vagabond Song.' Something about the language, the emphasis, the lyric quality, though he was considered a 'light verse-maker.' But it was his work that inspired me to pay more attention to the genre of poetry. ... Carman was where it started."[26] That same "open road" called out to George Elliott Clarke. Clarke hails from Windsor, Nova Scotia. This is next door to the site of Carman's great poem "Low Tide on Grand Pré." Clarke says he "couldn't help but be attracted to Carman's take on loss and sorrow and regret, the salt tears and salt tide and twilight (of everything)." Clarke "also appreciated Carman's pre-Beat (or maybe Tennysonian Beat) shtick of 'Vagabondia,' the title of a popular book of verse that Carman co-authored with Richard

Hovey, and which was influential for Ezra Pound; the volume celebrates the idea of rambling, the open road …"[27]

Finally, we come to the "Father of Canadian Literature," Sir Charles G.D. Roberts, the last Canadian poet to be knighted. It is an honour he deserved because Roberts got things going in 1880 with his first collection of poems. And his inspiration persists over a hundred and forty years later among the poets of today. It was Roberts, his two cousins Bliss Carman and Barry Bliss Straton, John Frederic Herbin, and Sophia M. Almon Hensley who put the Bay of Fundy on our literary map. All would write unforgettable poems of the natural beauty of the bay and the parts of New Brunswick and Nova Scotia it graces. In the case of Carman, his "Low Tide on Grand Pré," and in the case of Roberts, his "Tantramar Revisited" and "The Tide on Tantramar" live on as masterworks.

There are several poets today living on, or near, the Bay of Fundy on either its New Brunswick or Nova Scotia side, and celebrating its power and beauty in their books, for both shores are geographically striking and rich in history. It's to be expected that both Roberts and Carman will speak to them. One such poet is the aforementioned Margaret Patricia Eaton. Indeed, Roberts and his "Tantramar Revisited" stood in the background while she wrote the poetry that would become her *Painted Poems* and *Vision & Voice*.

Although there are many examples in her poetry of her debt to Roberts, here is one she selected. "In particular see the poem 'Pencils' page 10 in *Vision & Voice*—the narrative in this poem is personal—I am the person trying to decide whether to dwell in memory or move forward with my life and the yellow pencil in my suede jacket pocket is a metaphor for me to continue writing—however, the road I am walking on, The Stagecoach Road, passes by St. Ann's Anglican Church in British Settlement where Roberts' father was rector and where the family lived. So when this poem came to me, I was actually walking on that road in the autumn … and Angelica did the painting … she didn't do it because of Roberts but just because she was doing *plein aire* painting and liked to have someone around her when sitting in [an] isolated spot …"[28]

Eaton goes on to draw our attention to how the poetry of these early writers helped shape the collective memory of us as Canadians. The first books by our five poets of the Maritimes appeared during the exciting thirteen-year period of 1880 to 1893.[29] To return to Eaton's first letter of May 8, 2020, quoted above, "I'm not sure how much I consciously thought about Roberts and Carman's influence when writing those poems—but I think there was something unconsciously going on with them—stylistically in terms of imagery, in terms of collective memory and also in their view of the universe and our place in it. I believe there are transcendental influences in their work and I think there is some of that in mine ..."

The comments above from contemporary Canadian poets exclude any mention of Duncan Campbell Scott, one of the major voices of the period. Although Scott did not start the infamous Residential School system (*circ.* 1880–1996), now understood to have been racist, he did administer the program once he was elevated to the role of Deputy Superintendent General in 1913. Because of these schools, as well as his work on Treaty No. 9, Scott has fallen from grace. His poetry is no longer read. To show this shift in public opinion, in 1957 when C.F. Klinck and R.E. Watters published the revised edition of their *Canadian Anthology*,[30] the fact that Scott worked at Indian Affairs is merely mentioned in passing. The two editors note this work, and the travelling involved, led to some of Scott's nature poetry. By 1982 when Jack David and Robert Lecker brought out their anthology *Canadian Poetry*,[31] Kathy Mezei in her piece on Scott goes into greater detail. Professor Mezei states: "Since Scott as Deputy Superintendent of Indian Affairs apparently contributed to their demise and assimilation through his policies, the pathos and beauty of his poems portraying the Indian torn between two worlds seem paradoxical."[32] In her biographical sketch no mention is made of Residential Schools. She does note that Scott's great poem "The Height of Land" could not have been written if not for the poet's trips to northern Indigenous communities. But in the present century, much more has to be said concerning Treaty No. 9, the Residential Schools, and other policies developed by Indian

Affairs during Scott's tenure. (And, in fact, more has been said.[33]) That Scott is not read is both understandable and unfortunate.

Although Scott is responsible for some of the oppression of Indigenous children via the Residential Schools while he worked as an administrator at Indian Affairs, he is presented here as a *poet.* And as a poet he wrote exceedingly well. Although Scott wrote about the Indigenous Peoples and the North, as in "The Height of Land," he was not limited to those two topics. Here is his "Autumn Song,"[34] a poem that displays another side of Duncan Campbell Scott: a poet of great descriptive force.

Autumn Song

Sing me a song of the Autumn clear,
  With the mellow days and the ruddy eves;
Sing me a song of the ending year,
  With the piled-up sheaves.

Sing me a song of the apple bowers,
  Of the great grapes the vine-field yields,
Of the ripe peaches bright as flowers,
  And the rich hop-fields.

Sing me a song of the fallen mast,
  Of the sharp odour the pomace sheds,
Of the purple beets left last
  In the garden beds.

Sing me a song of the toiling bees,
  Of the long flight and the honey won,
Of the white hives under the apple-trees
  In the hazy sun.

Sing me a song of the thyme and the sage,
Of sweet-marjoram in the garden grey
Where goes my love Armitage
Pulling the summer savory.

Sing me a song of the red deep,
The long glow the sun leaves.
Of the swallows taking a last sleep
In the barn eaves.

I would encourage readers to revisit the poetry of Duncan Campbell Scott. He celebrated the beauty of Canada in poems like "Autumn Song." And perhaps more than any other Confederation Poet, Scott experimented with Modernism.

The point of this book has not been to air my views on the poets of the Confederation Period, although I have done that. Nor is this study intended to promote the ideas of others, however useful their ideas may be. My goal is simply to encourage you, the reader, to directly examine the poets covered within these pages, not by reading books about them, but *by reading their books*. It is your opinion that counts. There are two chief reasons to read the Confederation Poets: to understand the history of Canadian culture and for the pure joy of reading good poetry. Their poetry *is* a joy. And, in the end, it is the pleasure granted by a well-made text that matters most.

When we read their books we may receive something defining —something that marks us as Canadians—like the poets quoted in this Epilogue. Or we may have received something *indirectly* (or second hand, so to speak) through the poets the Confederation Poets knew and directly influenced. Most of the major Canadian poets of the 20th century drew deeply on the Confederation Poets. Dorothy Livesay did research on Isabella Valancy Crawford. The young Al Purdy saw himself as the Bliss Carman of his generation. Raymond Souster was inspired by the poetry of Archibald Lampman and Wilfred Campbell. Milton Acorn, like Souster, revered Archibald Lampman. And Pauline Johnson inspired, and continues to inspire, Indigenous poets across the nation. (Indeed, Johnson's poetry also influences many non-Indigenous poets.) This secondary influence has been the experience of contemporary poets as diverse as Robert Acorn, Robert Currie, G. W. Down, Gertrude Olga Down, Bernadette Gabay Dyer, David Haskins, Donna Langevin, Carol Malyon, John Reibetanz, Glen Sorestad, and J. J. Steinfeld. A notable example of how cultural history is passed on would be the Cree poet Sky Dancer (also known as Louise Bernice Halfe), Canada's recently appointed Parliamentary Poet Laureate. Her work, drawing from Indigenous history, and especially the culture of the people of the Prairies, influences Native and non-Native poets today.[35]

No matter how readers today experience their ideals, the works of our 19th century poets helped shape our Canadian consciousness in a lasting way. And in turn, this really goes back to Charles Sangster, Canada's first "National Poet," whose poetry and vision for Canada influenced the Confederation Poets. Following Sangster, each of our poets had to discover The True North. Each vision was unique, and yet each vision had common roots. But far beyond the value of their visions for their new nation, they are read today for the craft and beauty of their poems.

Notes

Author's Introduction: *The Tory In Every Woodlot*

1. Although the term Red Tory was coined by Gad Horowitz and used by and about Canadian philosopher and political scientist George Grant during the 1960s, it can be usefully employed to describe the cultural, social, religious, and political movements—in fact, the climate of opinion or *Zeitgeist*—that led to the creation and early development of Canada during the last four decades of the 19th century. While the Fathers of Confederation were certainly not all what we might today call "Red Tories," this was a leading force, and led to Sir John A. Macdonald becoming our initial Prime Minister. The Red Tory climate of opinion upon which Canada was established can be experienced best by reading the Poets of Confederation.
2. Richard Hooker (1554–1600) was a priest of the Church of England and a leading theologian in the 16th century. His major work was *Of the Laws of Ecclesiastical Polity.*
3. Benjamin Disraeli (1804–1881) was twice Prime Minister of Britain. His political battles with the Liberal William Ewart Gladstone are the stuff of legend.
4. Sir John A. (Alexander) Macdonald (1815–1891) was twice Prime Minister of Canada. As our first Prime Minister (1867–1873) he is considered to be the chief Father of Confederation.
5. It has been stated that Canada came into being in reaction to the American Civil War. It is the opinion of the present writer that even without the Civil War, Canada was well on the road to becoming a nation. At best, the War in the U.S. accelerated this process.

6. The eight major poets of the Confederation Period, and the titles and publication dates of their initial books, are: Wilfred Campbell (1858–1918), *Snowflakes and Sunbeams*, 1888; Bliss Carman (1861–1929), *Low Tide on Grand Pré: A Book of Lyrics*, 1893; Isabella Valancy Crawford (1850–1887), *Old Spookses' Pass, Malcolm's Katie, and Other Poems*, 1884; E. Pauline Johnson (1861–1913), *The White Wampum*, 1895; Archibald Lampman (1861–1899), *Among the Millet, and Other Poems*, 1888; Sir Charles G.D. Roberts (1860–1943), *Orion, and Other Poems*, 1880; Duncan Campbell Scott (1862–1947), *The Magic House, and Other Poems*, 1893; and Frederick George Scott (1861–1944), *Justin, and Other Poems*, 1885.
7. John (George) Diefenbaker (1895–1979) was Prime Minister of Canada from 1957 to 1963. Diefenbaker led the "social justice" wing of the Progressive Conservative Party of Canada and, among other things, worked to extend the right to vote to all Indigenous people. The foremost People's Poet, Milton Acorn, supported Diefenbaker when he stood up for Canada against then U.S. President John F. Kennedy.
8. A fuller selection of the Poets of Confederation may be obtained by consulting this re-issued anthology. Campbell, Wilfred, ed. *The Oxford Book of Canadian Verse*. Toronto: Oxford University Press, 1913. Re-issued with a new "Introduction" by Len Early in 2013. Print. Mr. Campbell's editorial choices are, however, not the most useful.
9. Christian, William and Colin Campbell. *Political Parties and Ideologies in Canada: Liberals, Conservatives, Socialists, Nationalists*. Toronto: McGraw-Hill Ryerson, 3rd edition, 1990. Print.
10. Lighthall, William Douw, ed. *Songs of the Great Dominion: Voices from the Forests and Waters, the Settlements and Cities of Canada*. London: Walter Scott, "Windsor Series," 1889. Print.
11. Atwood, Margaret, ed. *The New Oxford Book of Canadian Verse in English*. Toronto: Oxford University Press, 1982. pp. 35–37. Print.
12. In his unpublished paper, "'Canadian Born': Pauline Johnson's Affirmation of the True North in the Crisis of Atlantic Civilization," Terry Barker makes the point that Johnson was part

of the Red Tory culture of her time, the same as the other poets of the Confederation Period.

13. Thomas Hardy abandoned fiction for poetry after his novel *Jude the Obscure* was published at the close of the Victorian Period. John Masefield published his *Salt Water Ballads* in 1902, four years before Coleman's *Songs and Sonnets.*
14. The Group of Seven included the painters Franklin Carmichael (1890–1945), Lawren Harris (1885–1970), A.Y. Jackson (1882–1974), Frank Johnston (1888–1949), Arthur Lismer (1885–1969), J.E.H. MacDonald (1873–1932), and Frederick Varley (1881–1969). Tom Thomson (1877–1917), although usually associated with the group, was not a member.
15. Recent collections by the eight major poets are: Wilfred Campbell, *William Wilfred Campbell: Selected Poetry and Essays.* Boone, Laurel, ed. Waterloo, Ontario: Wilfrid Laurier University Press, 1987; Bliss Carman, *Windflower: Poems of Bliss Carman.* Souster, Raymond and Douglas Lochhead, eds. Ottawa: Tecumseh Press, 1985; Isabella Valancy Crawford, *The Collected Poems of Isabella Valancy Crawford.* Garvin, John, ed. Toronto: William Briggs, 1905. Reprinted with a new "Introduction" by James Reaney. Toronto: University of Toronto Press, 1972; E. Pauline Johnson, *E. Pauline Johnson, Tekahionwake: Collected Poems and Selected Prose.* Gerson, Carole and Veronica Strong-Boag, eds. Toronto: University of Toronto Press, 2002; Archibald Lampman, *Selected Poetry of Archibald Lampman.* Gnarowski, Michael, ed. Ottawa: Tecumseh Press, 1990; Sir Charles G.D. Roberts, *Collected Poems of Sir Charles G.D. Roberts.* Pacey, Desmond and Graham Adams, eds. Wolfville, Nova Scotia: Wombat Press, 1985; Duncan Campbell Scott, *Powassan's Drum: Poems of Duncan Campbell Scott.* Souster, Raymond and Douglas Lochhead, eds. Ottawa: Tecumseh Press, 1985; and Frederick George Scott, *Collected Poems.* Vancouver: Clarke & Stuart Co., 1934. (Works by the other poets are even more difficult to find.)

Charles Sangster:
Pre-Confederation Mystic

Five poetry collections by Charles Sangster:

The St. Lawrence and the Saguenay, and Other Poems. Kingston, C.W. [Canada West]: John Creighton and John Duff, 1856 and New York: Miller, Orton & Mulligan, 1856. Print. The title poem is composed of 110 nine-line Spenserian stanzas with nine lyric poems interspersed. The lyric poems are "Lyric to the Isles," "Hymn to the Lightning," "Twilight Hymn," "Canzonet," "The Whippoorwill," "Parting Song," "P.ean [should read: Paean] to the Dawn," "Vanished Hopes," and "Song."

A PDF of *The St. Lawrence and the Saguenay, and Other Poems* is available from: HathiTrust (www.hathitrust.org).

Hesperus and Other Poems and Lyrics. Montreal: J. Lovell, 1860. Print.

Our Norland. Toronto: Copp Clark, n.d. Print. This is a chapbook.

Norland Echoes and Other Strains and Lyrics. Frank M. Tierney, ed. Ottawa: Tecumseh Press, 1976. Print.

The Angel Guest and Other Poems and Lyrics. Frank M. Tierney, ed. Ottawa: Tecumseh Press, 1977. Print.

1. Sangster, Charles. "The St. Lawrence and the Saguenay." *The St. Lawrence and the Saguenay, and Other Poems*. Kingston, C.W. [Canada West]: John Creighton and John Duff, 1856 and New York: Miller, Orton & Mulligan, 1856. Print.
2. See the poem "At Levis Where the Current Meets the Tide." Acorn, Milton. *Jackpine Sonnets*. Toronto: Steel Rail Educational Publishing, 1977. p. 70. Print. Distinguishing Atlantic (or salt water) Canada from inland (or fresh water) Canada was important to Milton Acorn, as it was for the early French settlers for whom the rugged shore of the Gulf of St. Lawrence was a different

territory from the more lush, and far less harsh, St. Lawrence River lowlands of the Québec City/Trois-Rivières/Montréal region. The often rocky and unfriendly Gulf shoreline was settled first by the French, the river's more fertile banks were settled later.

3. Lac Saint-Jean was called Piekuakami in the Innu-aimun language at the time French explorers arrived. Lac Saint-Jean is the subject/site of myth and legend.
4. Sangster, Charles. *The St. Lawrence and the Saguenay, and Other Poems*. The title poem is written largely in nine-line Spenserian stanzas, following the practice of the English poet Edmund Spenser (1552–1599). This poem is on pages 9 to 61.
5. Sangster, Charles. "The St. Lawrence and the Saguenay." *The St. Lawrence and the Saguenay, and Other Poems*. Kingston, C.W. [Canada West]: John Creighton and John Duff, 1856 and New York: Miller, Orton & Mulligan, 1856. p. 10. Print.
6. *ibid*. p. 29.
7. *ibid*. p. 50.
8. Although Sangster travels through the traditional lands of the Iroquois, Algonquin, and Innu Peoples, the only tribe he names in his poem is the Têtes-de-Boule. (Today they are known as the Atikamekw People.) This group lived in the boreal forests of the upper Saint-Maurice River valley. The source of the Saint-Maurice River is at the Gouin Reservoir, located at the same latitude as Lac Saint-Jean, the centre of the Kingdom of Saguenay myth. (In 1535 Jacques Cartier named the Saint-Maurice the Rivière de Fouez.)

Sangster's personal mythology was a mixture of mystical Christianity, ancient Greek myth, and what little he was able to pick up by reading about the beliefs of Indigenous Canadians. This formed his vision of Canada. It was, however, principally Christian. Sangster did, like Duncan Campbell Scott fifty years later, think that the Indigenous tribes had a special relationship with the land. It is interesting that the Têtes-de-Boule play a role here since the boreal forests are quite far from Ottawa, Kingston, and Montréal.

9. It seems likely that Sangster had the legend of the Kingdom of Saguenay in mind when he wrote his poem. This legend, in its French-language version, first turns up in the 1530s and is associated with the voyages of the explorer Jacques Cartier. By the late 1500s news of this supposed "Canadian Arcadia" was also known to English mapmakers. One example of a British cartographer mentioning the mythical Kingdom of Saguenay is cited by Donald S. Johnson in his *Charting the Sea of Darkness*. New York: TAB Books, McGraw-Hill, 1993. Print. Johnson discusses a map made by Michael Lok, of London, England, that was published in 1582.

   Today the Saguenay and Lac Saint-Jean are major tourist destinations because of the extraordinary beauty of the region.
10. Brown, E.K. *On Canadian Poetry*. Toronto: McGraw-Hill Ryerson, 1943. Print. Reprinted in 1973 by Tecumseh Press. p. 33. Print.
11. Keats, John. "Ode on a Grecian Urn," quoted from Gayley, Charles Mills, C.C. Young, and Benjamin Putnam Kurtz, eds. *English Poetry: Its Principles and Progress*. New York: The Macmillan Company, 1920. pp. 257–259. Print.
12. Sangster, Charles. "The St. Lawrence and the Saguenay," Stanza VIII, Line 2.
13. Sangster never resolves the conflict between Christianity and Romanticism.
14. The Arcadian myth goes back no one knows how deeply into the dimness of antiquity. In this myth, Arcadia is a utopia. It is interesting that in the 16th century, Italian explorer Giovanni da Verrazzano named North America's Atlantic coast Arcadia.
15. Sangster, Charles. "The St. Lawrence and the Saguenay," Stanza XLIV, Lines 5–7.
16. The entire journey detailed in "The St. Lawrence and the Saguenay" takes place in the Canadian, or Precambrian, Shield. And the goal of Sangster's quest is the Lac Saint-Jean/Saguenay region of Québec, in the heart of the Shield.
17. This is not the place to set out the entire "plot" of this 52-page poem. Even a brief outline of "The St. Lawrence and the Saguenay" requires five pages.

18. The Laurentian Highlands of Québec is that area of the Shield between the Saguenay River in the east and the Gatineau River in the west. Much of this region is covered by boreal forests and lakes. It includes Lac Saint-Jean, the goal of Sangster's quest.
19. Latham, David. "Charles Sangster." *The Oxford Companion to Canadian Literature.* Toronto: Oxford University Press, 1983. pp. 727–728. Print.
20. Conway, Don. "Charles Sangster." *Canadian Poetry, Volume One.* Toronto: General Publishing, 1982. pp. 277–278. Print.
21. Tierney, Frank M. "Charles Sangster." *Dictionary of Canadian Biography*, Volume XII (1891-1900). Toronto and Québec: University of Toronto and Université Laval, 1966.
22. Sangster, Charles. "The Indian Summer." *The St. Lawrence and the Saguenay, and Other Poems.* p. 204. Print.
23. Alt, Marlene. "Charles Sangster." *The Canadian Encyclopedia.* Edmonton: Hurtig Publishers, 1985. p. 1633. Print.
24. Sangster, Charles. "Canzonet." *The St. Lawrence and the Saguenay, and Other Poems.* p. 28. Print.
25. Sangster, Charles. "A Northern Rune." Campbell, Wilfred, ed. *The Oxford Book of Canadian Verse.* Toronto: Oxford University Press, 1913. pp. 34–35. Print. Also in: Sangster, Charles. *Norland Echoes and Other Strains and Lyrics.* Ottawa: Tecumseh Press, 1976. pp. 31–33. Print.
26. Hyperborea was commonly associated in Canada with the Kingdom of Saguenay. While Charles Sangster was interested in legends concerning Arcadia, Hyperborea, and, quite possibly, the Kingdom of Saguenay, there is no indication that the Confederation Poets shared this interest. They were not looking to Québec for meaning. Nor were they, but for a few exceptions, looking to Indigenous traditions. Although they knew each other from working at the Post Office Department in Ottawa, the world Archibald Lampman was seeking was not the world explored by Charles Sangster.
27. The New Jerusalem is to be the fulfilment of God's will on earth. See: "The Book of Revelation," the final book of the *New*

Testament. The Puritans of New England also saw the New World as a possible site of a New Jerusalem.

28. Ross, Malcolm. *The Impossible Sum of Our Traditions*. Toronto: McClelland and Stewart, 1986. pp. 191–192. Print.
29. McLay, Catherine M., ed. *Canadian Literature: the beginnings to the 20th century*. Toronto: McClelland and Stewart, 1974. p. 190. Print.

The Bay of Fundy and its Tantramar Marshes: ***The Beginning of a Canadian Literature***

In addition to his wonderful poem on the Fundean marshlands, "Evening on the Marshes," quoted in my text, Barry Bliss Straton wrote vivid poems purely about the natural beauty of his native region. Here is one example:

The Silver Frost

A breath from the tropics broke Winter's spell
With an alien rain which froze as it fell,
And ere the Orient blushed with morn
A beautiful crystal forest was born.

Blackthorn hedge and hawthorn bush
Dawned spectrally white in the first grey flush;
Drifted from night the circling trees
As icebergs drift from northern seas.

Branch above branch, an aerial maze
Of pendulous crystals and silver sprays!
Tree behind tree impregnable,
Where beauty, and silence, and sweet thoughts dwell!

The elm boughs bend, like a searching thought,
With their silvery weight of beauty caught.
White limbs are asleep on the misty blue skies
Like lilies on lakelets in paradise.

Daylight refulgent floods over the hills,
And the forest, conscious of beauty, thrills;
Through the mazes of fragile mimicry
The dazzling sunrays flare and flee.

Pine, elm, and maple, in icy attire,
Burn with a myriad gems of fire;
The snow-billowed ground and the gossamer height
Are aflame with the scornful spirit of light.

Violet, orange, indigo, red,
Green, yellow, and blue from each diamond are shed;
More beautiful these than the jewels of a throne,
For the forest is nature's glory and crown.

The grape-vine over the lilacs laid
Gleams like a rainbow, tossed cascade,
And he who beholds might pause to hear
The enlivened voices of waters there.

In the Balm of Gilead and poplar's spire
Are incarnate the spirits of water and fire;
In cedar and linden, and everywhere,
The flames of the passionless fires flare.

But wandering winds the frail boughs shake,
And rustling ripples of ruin awake,
And a myriad scintillant gems fall down,
Like thoughts transfigured of beauty flown.

From: Lighthall, William Douw, ed. *Songs of the Great Dominion: Voices from the Forests and Waters, the Settlements and Cities of Canada.* London: Walter Scott, "Windsor Series," 1889. pp. 409–410. Print.

1. Both of these poems will be discussed later in this book.
2. Straton, Barry. *Lays of Love, and Miscellaneous Poems.* Saint John, New Brunswick: J. & A. McMillan, 1884. Print. Having been born on December 27, 1854, Barry Bliss Straton was six years older than Sir Charles G.D. Roberts and seven years older than Bliss Carman. It is possible that his cousins were inspired to write about the marshlands by Straton's own poetry.
3. Lighthall, William Douw, ed. *Songs of the Great Dominion: Voices from the Forests and Waters, the Settlements and Cities of Canada.* London: Walter Scott, "Windsor Series," 1889. Print.
4. Rand, Theodore H., ed. *A Treasury of Canadian Verse.* London: J.M. Dent, 1900 and Toronto: William Briggs, 1900. Print. Straton appears here with 13 fellow Confederation Poets who are covered in the present study: G.F. Cameron, B. Carman, I.V. Crawford, S.F. Harrison, S.M.A. Hensley, J.F. Herbin, E.P. Johnson, A. Lampman, W.D. Lighthall, C.G.D. Roberts, D.C. Scott, F.G. Scott, and E. Wetherald.
5. Burpee, Lawrence J., ed. *A Century of Canadian Sonnets.* Toronto: The Musson Book Company, 1910. Print. Straton appears here with 10 fellow Confederation Poets who are covered in the present study: G.F. Cameron, W. Campbell, B. Carman, H. Coleman, S.F. Harrison, S.M.A. Hensley, J.F. Herbin, W.D. Lighthall, F.G. Scott, and E. Wetherald.
6. See: Lochhead, Douglas. *High Marsh Road: Lines for a Diary.* Toronto: Anson-Cartwright Editions, 1980. Print. And also: Lochhead, Douglas. *Weathers: Poems New and Selected.* Fredericton, New Brunswick: Goose Lane Editions, 2002. Print.
7. See: Thompson, John. *At the Edge of the Chopping There are No Secrets.* Toronto: House of Anansi, 1973. Print. And also: Thompson, John. *Collected Poems and Translations.* Fredericton, New Brunswick: Goose Lane Editions, 1995. Print.
8. Straton, Barry. "Evening on the Marshes." *Lays of Love, and Miscellaneous Poems.* Saint John, New Brunswick: J. & A. McMillan, 1884. pp. 71–72. Print. *Lays of Love, and Miscellaneous Poems* has been made available online by: HathiTrust (www.hathitrust.org).

Sir Charles G.D. Roberts:
Poet of the Tantramar

While Sir Charles G.D. Roberts published many collections, and all contain good poems, his finest single volume would be *Songs of the Common Day* (1893). It offers 37 of his celebrated sonnets along with longer pieces. Also important is *In Divers Tones* (1886). Much of his best poetry is found in these two early books.

1. Roberts, Charles G.D. *Orion, and Other Poems*. Philadelphia: J.B. Lippincott & Co., 1880. Print.
2. Roberts, Charles G.D. *In Divers Tones*. Boston: D. Lothrop and Company, 1886. Print. This collection contains "The Sower." (Quoted in the text.)
3. Roberts, Charles G.D. *Songs of the Common Day*. London and New York: Longmans, Green, and Co., 1893. Print. Facsimile edition by Bibliolife (Bibliolife, P.O. Box 21206, Charleston, South Carolina, 29413, U.S.A.). Print. This collection contains "The Herring Weir." (Quoted in the text.) See page 29.
4. Almost always overlooked is the influence of the American poet Sidney Lanier (1842–1881). *In Divers Tones* contains a couple of poems—"To the Memory of Sidney Lanier" and "On Reading the Poems of Sidney Lanier"—that show Roberts' debt to Lanier. In "To the Memory of Sidney Lanier" he calls the older American poet "My Elder Brother." In "On Reading the Poems of Sidney Lanier" Roberts writes:

   Poet and Flute-player, that flute of thine
   To me must ever seem thy perfect sign!
   Tho' strenuously with breath divine inspired,
   To thy strait law is due thy deathless line.

It is well worth comparing the Roberts poems "Tantramar Revisited" and "The Tide on Tantramar" with Lanier's "The Marshes of Glynn." Although this book is not the place to do so, it could be argued that Roberts made a true spiritual and literary connection with Sidney Lanier, and not simply because they both wrote great poems about marshes. For one thing, they both wrote elegiacally of the passing of a cherished world and lamented a lost innocence. They also struggled to overcome their own imperfections.

Roberts' affinity with Lanier might explain why Wordsworth's Lake District nature poetry—a definite influence on Roberts—is celebratory, while Roberts' own nature poetry is more sombre. There is a feeling of impending loss in Roberts not commonly experienced in early Wordsworth. I believe this adds greater depth to the poetry of Roberts.

By the way, *In Divers Tones* also contains "To S____ M____," a love poem to his fellow Confederation Poet Sophie M. (Margaretta) Almon Hensley. This could cast some light on the cause of the breakup of Roberts' marriage in 1897. It is known that he had at least an "affair of the heart" with her, and this poem suggests it might have been more than that.

5. Roberts, Charles G.D. *Canada Speaks of Britain and Other Poems of the War*. Toronto: Ryerson Press, 1941. Print.
6. See, for example: "Cambrai and Marne" and "Going Over." *New Poems*. London: Constable, 1919. Print.
7. See, for example: "In a City Room," "Twilight on Sixth Avenue," and "At the Railway Station." *New York Nocturnes, and Other Poems*. Boston: Lamson, Wolffe, 1898. Print. And also, "Heat in the City" and "The Great and the Little Weavers." *The Book of the Rose*. Boston: Page, 1903. Print.
8. Decades after Roberts left the Tantramar/Bay of Fundy region, he still wrote poems set in the marshland. "Westcock Hill" was included in his collection *The Iceberg and Other Poems* (1934). And in 1955 when Desmond Pacey edited *The Selected Poems of Sir Charles G.D. Roberts*, Pacey chose "Westcock Hill" to close the volume. In this poem Roberts writes about "My memoried Tantramar"

and its "turbid floods" and "The salt tang and the buckwheat scents" of his childhood home.

9. It is interesting to compare Roberts' "Tantramar Revisited" (1883) and Carman's "Low Tide on Grand Pré" (first version as "Low Tide on Avon" in 1886, final version as "Low Tide on Grand Pré" in 1887).
10. Emerson, Ralph Waldo. *Nature*. Boston: James Munroe and Company, 1836. Print.
11. Roberts, Charles G.D. "The Unsleeping." *The Book of the Native*. Toronto: Copp, Clark Company, 1896. Print.

Isabella Valancy Crawford: *Poet of a Nation's Thanks*

1. It is not certain how many children the Crawfords had, nor is it clear how many accompanied Mrs. Crawford to Canada. (Several had died in Ireland.) It seems there were at least a dozen children, and probably thirteen. Birth and death records were poorly kept in the 19th century. Reportedly, seven died during a single week in 1855. Only one, Stephen Walter Crawford, would marry and produce offspring. Most of the others did not survive childhood, and Isabella did not marry.
2. Atwood, Margaret, ed. *The New Oxford Book of Canadian Verse in English.* Toronto: Oxford University Press, 1982. pp. 19–24. Print. Atwood dates these poems as 1880 (The Camp of Souls), 1883 (The Dark Stag), and 1884 (Said the Canoe), placing them within Crawford's Toronto years.
3. Crawford's eroticism was noted by Robert Alan Burns. See: his piece "Isabella Valancy Crawford." *Canadian Poetry, Volume One.* Toronto: General Publishing, 1982. pp. 278–280. Print.

In his study *Isabella Valancy Crawford and Her Works* (Toronto: ECW Press, n.d.), Burns notes that Crawford changed line 46 of "The Lily Bed" from "Their soft clasp to the frail sides sprang," (as quoted in my text) to "Their soft palms to the pale sides sprang," thus "making more definite the suggestion of human sexual excitement." (J.W. Garvin, however, went with the original in his *The Collected Poems of Isabella Valancy Crawford,* as did Elizabeth McNeill Galvin in her *Isabella Valancy Crawford: We Scarcely Knew Her.*)

4. Crawford, Isabella Valancy. "The Lily Bed." *The Evening Telegram* [Toronto] 30 October 1884: 4. Print. In this study I have used

The Collected Poems of Isabella Valancy Crawford as my copy-text for Crawford's poetry because this was the best-known version for many decades even though some changes were made to the poems since they were first published during the poet's lifetime.

5. "The Lily Bed" can also be found in: Garvin, J.W., ed. *The Collected Poems of Isabella Valancy Crawford*. Toronto: William Briggs, 1905. pp. 169–171. Print. This book was reprinted, with a new "Introduction" by James Reaney, as *Collected Poems*. Toronto: University of Toronto Press, 1972. Print.

"The Lily Bed" also appears in: David, Jack and Robert Lecker, eds. *Canadian Poetry, Volume One*. Toronto: General Publishing, 1982. pp. 50–52. Print.

A third version of "The Lily Bed" appears in: Galvin, Elizabeth McNeill. *Isabella Valancy Crawford: We Scarcely Knew Her*. Toronto: Natural Heritage/Natural History, 1994. pp. 100–102. Print. These three versions are different from each other, and are different from the poem as published in *The Evening Telegram*.

Each of these versions has its attractive features as well as its flaws, and the one in *Canadian Poetry, Volume One* might be close to the spelling and punctuation of the Crawford original. (I have, however, used the version in *The Collected Poems of Isabella Valancy Crawford*.) Scholars of Crawford should, of course, consult all versions of this major poem.

6. Crawford, Isabella Valancy. *Fairy Tales of Isabella Valancy Crawford*. Petrone, Penny, ed. Ottawa: Borealis Press, 1977. Print.
7. Crawford, Isabella Valancy. *Selected Stories of Isabella Valancy Crawford*. Petrone, Penny, ed. Ottawa: University of Ottawa Press, 1975. Print.
8. Crawford, Isabella Valancy. "Canada to England." *The Collected Poems of Isabella Valancy Crawford*. Toronto: William Briggs, 1905. pp. 236–238. Print.
9. Traill, Catharine Parr. *The Backwoods of Canada: Being Letters from the Wife of an Emigrant Officer, Illustrative of the Domestic Economy of British America*. London: Charles Knight, The Library of Entertaining Knowledge, 1836. Print.

10. The relationship between the writings of Catharine Parr Traill and those of Isabella Valancy Crawford is discussed quite fully in Burns, Robert Alan. *Isabella Valancy Crawford and Her Works.* Toronto: ECW Press, n.d. Print.
11. Crawford, Isabella Valancy. "The Inspiration of Song." *The Favorite* 15 February 1873. Print. See: Garvin, pp. 58–60.
12. Crawford, Isabella Valancy. "The Vesper Star." *The Mail* [Toronto] 24 December 1873: 3. Print. See: Garvin, p. 253.
13. Crawford, Isabella Valancy. "Wealth." See: Garvin, pp. 85–86.
14. The idea of "wage-slavery" did not originate with Karl Marx. It goes back to the writings of Cicero, where Crawford likely encountered it in her father's library.
15. Seranus [Susan Frances Harrison] is quoted in "Great Poetess Buried in Little Lake Cemetery" by "Jeanette." *Peterborough Examiner* 20 March 1934. Print.
16. Crawford, Isabella Valancy. "The Rose of a Nation's Thanks." See: Garvin, pp. 45–47.
17. Crawford, Isabella Valancy. "Canada to England." See: Garvin, pp. 236–238.

Frederick George Scott: *Poet of the Laurentians*

1. Scott, Frederick George. *Poems Old and New.* London: Society for Promoting Christian Knowledge, 1936. Print.
2. Scott, Frederick George. "The Unnamed Lake." *The Unnamed Lake, and Other Poems.* Toronto: William Briggs, 1897. Print.
3. Scott, Frederick George. "The King's Bastion." *The Oxford Book of Canadian Verse.* Toronto: Oxford University Press, 1913. p. 211. Print. My copy-text is: *Collected Poems.* Vancouver: Clarke & Stuart, 1934. p. 57. Print.
4. Scott, Frederick George. *The Great War As I Saw It.* Toronto: F.D. Goodchild, 1922. Print. This book presents an unflinching view of some of the most extreme suffering and bravery at Ypres, the Somme, Vimy Ridge, Amiens, etc.
5. Scott, Frederick George. "In Memoriam." *The Oxford Book of Canadian Verse*, pp. 211–213. Print.
6. Scott, Frederick George. "Call Back Our Dead." This poem was initially published in *The New York Times.* My copy-text is: *Canadian Poetry: From the Beginnings Through the First World War.* Toronto: McClelland & Stewart, 1994. p. 333. Print.
7. Scott, Frederick George. "In the Woods." *The Oxford Book of Canadian Verse*, pp. 216–217. Print. My copy-text is: *Collected Poems.* Vancouver: Clarke & Stuart, 1934. p. 1. Print.
8. The stanzas from Scott's "The Unnamed Lake" are copied from *The New Oxford Book of Canadian Verse in English.* Toronto: Oxford University Press, 1982. pp. 46–47. Print.
9. Scott, Frederick George. *Collected Poems.* Vancouver: Clarke & Stuart, 1934. Print. All of the poems cited here, except "In Memoriam," are included.

George Frederick Cameron: *The Classic Poet*

1. Campbell, Wilfred, ed. *The Oxford Book of Canadian Verse.* Toronto: Oxford University Press, 1913. Print. Facsimile edition, with a new "Introduction" by Len Early, published by OUP in 2013. Print.
2. Lochhead, Douglas. "George Frederick Cameron." *The Oxford Companion to Canadian Literature.* Toronto: Oxford University Press, 1983. p. 99. Print.
3. Lampman, Archibald. "Two Canadian Poets: A Lecture, 1891." Smith, A.J.M., ed. *Masks of Poetry: Canadian Critics on Canadian Verse.* Toronto: McClelland and Stewart, 1962. pp. 26–44. Print.
4. Cameron, George Frederick. *Lyrics on Freedom, Love and Death.* Cameron, Charles J., ed. Printed by the *Daily News*, Kingston, Ontario, 1887. Print. Fortunately, Professor D.M.R. Bentley and *Canadian Poetry* have made these poems available at: www.canadianpoetry.ca/confederation/cameron/lyrics/index.htm
5. Cameron, George Frederick. "My Fate." *Lyrics on Freedom, Love and Death*, p. 289.
6. Cameron, George Frederick. "My Faith." *Lyrics on Freedom, Love and Death*, p. 189.
7. Cameron, George Frederick. "Standing on Tiptoe." *Lyrics on Freedom, Love and Death*, p. 136. Also, see: *The Oxford Book of Canadian Verse.* Toronto: Oxford University Press, 1913. p. 105. Print.
8. Keats, John. "Ode on a Grecian Urn." *English Poetry: Its Principles and Progress.* New York: The Macmillan Company, 1920. pp. 257–259. Print.

9. Douglas Lochhead states in his entry on Cameron in *The Oxford Companion to Canadian Literature* that the poet had read most of Virgil and Cicero in their original Latin prior to age fourteen. See: page 99.

William Douw Lighthall: *Poet of the Songs*

1. Lighthall, William Douw, ed. *Songs of the Great Dominion: Voices from the Forests and Waters, the Settlements and Cities of Canada.* London: Walter Scott, "Windsor Series," 1889. Print.
2. Lighthall included 1 poem by Cameron, 2 poems each by Harrison, Johnson, D.C. Scott, and F.G. Scott, 5 poems by Carman, 6 poems by both Crawford and Lampman, 7 poems by Lighthall himself, 12 poems by Campbell, and 13 poems by Roberts. This was the first gathering of our Confederation Poets.
3. Campbell, Wilfred, ed. *The Oxford Book of Canadian Verse.* Toronto: Oxford University Press, 1913. Print. Garvin, John W., ed. *Canadian Poets.* Toronto: McClelland, Goodchild & Stewart, 1916. Print.
4. A selection from Lighthall's introduction is included in: Smith, A.J.M., ed. *Masks of Poetry: Canadian Critics on Canadian Verse.* Toronto: McClelland and Stewart, 1962. pp. 17–25. Print.
5. This is not to suggest in any way that French and English Canadians would always get along, or that First Nations tribes and settlers would always get along. But some level of accommodation had to be reached for a Canadian People to emerge. Unfortunately, as time went on the culture and concerns of Indigenous Canadians were increasingly ignored by the government and by society in general. Due to government policies, these first Canadians became a marginalized people within their own country. Tragically, neglect and oppression continue to the present day.
6. It is interesting to note that Lighthall believed much of the best verse in American literary periodicals of his day to be by Canadian poets.

7. Carman, Bliss. "In Apple Time." *Low Tide on Grand Pré: A Book of Lyrics*. Cambridge & Chicago: Stone and Kimball, 1893. Print.
8. Purdy, Al. "Selling Apples." *To Paris Never Again*. Madeira Park, British Columbia: Harbour Publishing, 1997. pp. 69–73. Print. When a young poet in the 1940s, Al Purdy wanted to become the Bliss Carman of his generation. Instead, he became the Al Purdy of his generation.
9. Dewart, Edward Hartley, ed. *Selections from Canadian Poets*. Montreal: J. Lovell, 1864. Print. Reprinted by the University of Toronto Press in 1972. Print.
10. Gerson, Carole and Gwendolyn Davies, eds. *Canadian Poetry: From the Beginnings Through the First World War*. Toronto: McClelland & Stewart, 1994. pp. 369–370. Print.
11. Campbell, Wilfred, ed. *The Oxford Book of Canadian Verse*. Toronto: Oxford University Press, 1913. Print.
12. Lighthall, William Douw. "The Confused Dawn." *Thoughts, Moods and Ideals: Crimes of Leisure*. Montreal: "Witness" Printing House, 1887. Print. Fortunately, this book is available on-line through Project Gutenberg at: www.gutenberg.org/cache/epub/14616/pg14616.html

My copy-text, however, is: Lighthall, W.D. *Old Measures: Collected Verse*. Montreal: A.T. Chapman, 1922 and Toronto: The Musson Book Co., 1922. pp. 13–14. Print.

13. Lighthall, William Douw. "Montreal." *Thoughts, Moods and Ideals: Crimes of Leisure*. Montreal: "Witness" Printing House, 1887. Print.

My copy-text, however, is: Lighthall, W.D. *Old Measures: Collected Verse*. Montreal: A.T. Chapman, 1922 and Toronto: The Musson Book Co., 1922. p. 29. Print.

14. Lighthall, William Douw. "My Native Land." Rand, Theodore H., ed. *A Treasury of Canadian Verse*. London: J.M. Dent, 1900 and Toronto: William Briggs, 1900. pp. 186–187. Print.
15. Lighthall, William Douw. *Old Measures: Collected Verse*. Montreal: A.T. Chapman, 1922 and Toronto: The Musson Book Co., 1922. Print.

Archibald Lampman:
Poet on the Cusp of Modernism

The quote from Raymond Souster is from "Archibald Lampman: A Debt Repaid." Souster, Raymond, ed. *Comfort of the Fields*. Sutton West, Ontario: The Paget Press, 1979. p. xvi. Print.

1. Barker, Terry. "Tracking the True North." *Canadian Stories* 22.126 (2019) 64–66. Print.
2. Tennyson, Alfred. *Idylls of the King*. London: Edward Moxon & Co., 1859. Print. See the 1873 epilogue "To The Queen." The True North is cited in this epilogue, which had not been part of the original poem.
3. It is likely that Eduard Mörike inspired Lampman's fairy tale "Hans Fingerhut's Frog Lesson," collected in: Davies, Barrie, ed. *Archibald Lampman: Selected Prose*. Ottawa: Tecumseh Press, 1978. pp. 21–29. Print.
4. See the introduction to: Lighthall, William Douw, ed. *Songs of the Great Dominion: Voices from the Forests and Waters, the Settlements and Cities of Canada*. London: Walter Scott, "Windsor Series," 1889. Print. A selection from Lighthall's introduction is included in: Smith, A.J.M., ed. *Masks of Poetry: Canadian Critics on Canadian Verse*. Toronto: McClelland and Stewart, 1962. pp. 17–25. Print.
5. Early, L.R. *Archibald Lampman and His Works*. Toronto: ECW Press, n.d. Print.
6. In his youth, Lampman lived in areas such as Morpeth, Perrytown, Rice Lake, Cobourg, and Port Hope. He was educated at Trinity College, University of Toronto. As a lad from southern Ontario, he was not captivated by the Canadian wilderness until he moved to Ottawa following university graduation.

7. For a sample of the poems Lampman wrote for Katherine Waddell see: "A Portrait in Six Sonnets" collected in *At the Long Sault and Other New Poems*. Edited with a Foreword by Duncan Campbell Scott. Toronto: Ryerson Press, 1943. Print. Also see: Whitridge, Margaret Coulby, ed. *Lampman's Kate: Late Love Poems of Archibald Lampman, 1887–1897*. Ottawa: Borealis Press, 1975. Print.
8. Lampman, Archibald. "A Niagara Landscape." *The Poems of Archibald Lampman*. Toronto: George N. Morang, 1900. Print. Also included in *Comfort of the Fields*. Sutton West, Ontario: The Paget Press, 1979. p. 24. Print.
9. Lampman, Archibald. "Temagami." *The Poems of Archibald Lampman*. Toronto: George N. Morang, 1900. Print. Also included in *Comfort of the Fields*. Sutton West, Ontario: The Paget Press, 1979. p. 103. Print.
10. Lampman, Archibald. "In the Wilds." *The Poems of Archibald Lampman*. Toronto: George N. Morang, 1900. Print. Also included in *Comfort of the Fields*. Sutton West, Ontario: The Paget Press, 1979. p. 99. Print.
11. The Abbot Anthony quote is from *The Wisdom of the Desert*, translated by Thomas Merton. New York: New Directions, 1960. Print. See: Part CIII, p. 62.
12. Lampman, Archibald. "The City of the End of Things." *Alcyone*. Ottawa: James Ogilvy, 1899. Print. Also included in *Comfort of the Fields*. Sutton West, Ontario: The Paget Press, 1979. pp. 91–93. Print. This poem appears to be based on Hamilton, Ontario. Milton Acorn had this poem by memory and, like Raymond Souster, considered it to be among the finest poems of 19th century Canada.
13. Early, L.R. *Archibald Lampman and His Works*. Toronto: ECW Press, n.d. Print.
14. Souster, Raymond. "Archibald Lampman: A Debt Repaid." *Comfort of the Fields*. Sutton West, Ontario: The Paget Press, 1979. p. xvi. Print.

Wilfred Campbell:
Poet of the Lake Region

1. In 1913, Wilfred Campbell accepted four poems by the Duke—"Canada," "Quebec," "Qu'Appelle Valley," and "Alberta"—for *The Oxford Book of Canadian Verse*. See pages 73–78.
2. Campbell, Wilfred. *The Beauty, History, Romance and Mystery of the Canadian Lake Region*. Toronto: The Musson Book Co., 1910. Print. This is a non-fiction book. In general, the Lake Region refers to the Great Lakes Basin, but as used by Campbell the focus is on Lake Huron, Georgian Bay, and the Bruce Peninsula.
3. Campbell, Wilfred. "Lake Huron, October." *Lake Lyrics and Other Poems*. Saint John, New Brunswick: J. & A. McMillan, 1889. Print.
4. Campbell, Wilfred. "Indian Summer." *Snowflakes and Sunbeams*. St. Stephen, New Brunswick: *The Saint Croix Courier* Press, 1888. Print.
5. Campbell, Wilfred. "Morning on the Shore." *The Dread Voyage Poems*. Toronto: William Briggs, 1893. Print.
6. Davies, Barrie, ed. *At the Mermaid Inn: Wilfred Campbell, Archibald Lampman, Duncan Campbell Scott in* The Globe *1892–3*. Toronto: University of Toronto Press, 1979. Print.
7. Campbell, Wilfred. "The Tragedy of Man." *Sagas of Vaster Britain: Poems of the Race, the Empire and the Divinity of Man*. Toronto: The Musson Book Co., 1914. Print.
8. Campbell, Wilfred. *Beyond the Hills of Dream*. Boston: Houghton Mifflin, 1899. Print.
9. Campbell, Wilfred. *Sagas of Vaster Britain: Poems of the Race, the Empire and the Divinity of Man*. Toronto: The Musson Book Co., 1914. Print.

10. Campbell, Wilfred, ed. *The Oxford Book of Canadian Verse*. Toronto: Oxford University Press, 1913. Print. In his 1913 "Preface," Campbell is clear that, on the eve of the First World War, he privileged verse that upheld the "British ideals, traditions, religion, history, and heredity" of the men and women who established English-speaking Canada, to use his own words. At that time, most people living in English Canada (Campbell does not cover verse in French) had English, Scots, or Irish roots. The same can be said for the Fathers of Confederation.
11. Campbell, Wilfred. "The Winter Lakes." *Lake Lyrics and Other Poems*. Saint John, New Brunswick: J. & A. McMillan, 1889. Print.
12. Campbell, Wilfred. "How One Winter Came in the Lake Region." *The Dread Voyage Poems*. Toronto: William Briggs, 1893. Print.

Sophia M. Almon Hensley: *Poet of Romance*

1. Hensley, Sophia M. Almon (writing as Almon Hensley). "Slack Tide." *The Heart of a Woman*. New York: G.P. Putnam's Sons, 1906. pp. 106–107. Print.

Also in: Gerson, Carole and Gwendolyn Davies, eds. *Canadian Poetry: From the Beginnings Through the First World War*. Toronto: McClelland & Stewart, 1994. p. 292. Print.

2. Hensley, Sophia M. Almon (writing as Almon Hensley). "There Is No God." *The Heart of a Woman*. New York: G.P. Putnam's Sons, 1906. p. 166. Print.
3. Hensley, Sophia M. Almon (writing as Almon Hensley). "When Summer Comes." *The Heart of a Woman*. New York: G.P. Putnam's Sons, 1906. p. 175. Print.

Also in: Gerson, Carole and Gwendolyn Davies, eds. *Canadian Poetry: From the Beginnings Through the First World War*. Toronto: McClelland & Stewart, 1994. p. 291. Print.

4. While both Isabella Valancy Crawford and Hensley often wrote like modern women in terms of their choice of topics, Crawford led the quiet, retiring life of a Victorian maiden, not so Hensley.
5. Hensley, Sophia M. Almon (writing as Sophie M. Almon-Hensley). "Song." *A Woman's Love Letters*. New York: J. Selwyn Tait and Sons, 1895. pp. 76–77. Print.
6. David, Jack and Robert Lecker, eds. *Canadian Poetry, Volume One*. Toronto: General Publishing, 1982. Print. Not one Hensley poem is included.
7. Atwood, Margaret, ed. *The New Oxford Book of Canadian Verse in English*. Toronto: Oxford University Press, 1982. Print. Not one Hensley poem is included.

8. Eliot's *The Waste Land* was published in 1922 and Pound's *A Draft of XVI Cantos* in 1925. These books, along with James Joyce's *Ulysses* (1922), signalled the beginning of Modernism.
9. The first poetry collection by Al Purdy was *The Enchanted Echo* (Vancouver: Clarke & Stuart, 1944) and the first one by Raymond Souster was *When We Are Young* (Montreal: First Statement, 1945).

John Frederic Herbin: *Poet of the Acadian Diaspora*

1. Lampman, Archibald. "At The Mermaid Inn." *The Globe* [Toronto] 24 June 1893. Print. Lampman's book review is collected in: Campbell, Wilfred, Archibald Lampman, Duncan Campbell Scott. *At The Mermaid Inn: Wilfred Campbell, Archibald Lampman, Duncan Campbell Scott in* The Globe *1892-3*. Davies, Barrie, ed. Toronto: University of Toronto Press, 1979. pp. 335–336. Print.
2. Almost all Acadian writers, like Antonine Maillet, write and publish in French. Herbin's mother, Marie-Marguerite Robichaud, was Acadian and he identified with her and her people. His father, John Herbin, was a Huguenot who came to Canada from Cambrai, France.
3. The Acadian Diaspora/Le Grand Dérangement (1755–1763): The English military officer in charge of the Acadian Diaspora was Colonel John Winslow. He was assisted by Charles Morris, who developed the plan of action. It is interesting to note that Colonel Winslow was an ancestor of the American poet Robert Lowell (1917–1977). Once the Acadians were gone, Governor Charles Lawrence permitted their land to be taken over by settlers from the American colonies to the south.
4. Herbin, John Frederic. "The Marshlands." *The Marshlands: Souvenir in Song of the Land of Evangeline.* Windsor, Nova Scotia: J.J. Anslow, 1893. Print.

My copy-text for all of Herbin's poems is:

Herbin, John Frederic. *The Marshlands and The Trail of the Tide.* Toronto: William Briggs, 1899. Print.

5. Herbin, John Frederic. "An Acadian at Grand-Pré." *The Marshlands: Souvenir in Song of the Land of Evangeline.* Windsor, Nova Scotia:

J.J. Anslow, 1893. Print. This is the same year Bliss Carman published *Low Tide on Grand Pré: A Book of Lyrics*.

6. Herbin, John Frederic. "The Gaspereau." *The Marshlands: Souvenir in Song of the Land of Evangeline*. Windsor, Nova Scotia: J.J. Anslow, 1893. Print.
7. Herbin, John Frederic. "To The Singers of Minas." *The Marshlands: Souvenir in Song of the Land of Evangeline*. Windsor, Nova Scotia: J.J. Anslow, 1893. Print. In "To The Singers of Minas" reference is made to Roberts' poem "Tantramar Revisited" as well as to Carman's "Low Tide on Grand Pré."
8. Herbin, John Frederic. "Haying." *The Marshlands: Souvenir in Song of the Land of Evangeline*. Windsor, Nova Scotia: J.J. Anslow, 1893. Print.

Susan Frances Harrison: *The Poet who Looked to Québec*

1. Harrison, Susan Frances. *Crowded Out! And Other Sketches.* Ottawa: *The Evening Journal*, 1886. Print.
2. Harrison, Susan Frances (writing as S. Frances Harrison). *Pine, Rose, and Fleur de Lis.* Toronto: Hart & Company, 1890. Print.
3. Harrison, Susan Frances (writing as S. Frances Harrison). "Les Chantiers." *Pine, Rose, and Fleur de Lis.* Toronto: Hart & Company, 1890. p. 36. Print. Also see: Gerson, Carole and Gwendolyn Davies, eds. *Canadian Poetry: From the Beginnings Through the First World War.* Toronto: McClelland & Stewart, 1994. pp. 297–298. Print.
4. Harrison, Susan Frances (writing as S. Frances Harrison). "Château Papineau." Rand, Theodore H., ed. *A Treasury of Canadian Verse.* London: J.M. Dent, 1900 and Toronto: William Briggs, 1900. pp. 127–128. Print. My copy-text is *Pine, Rose, and Fleur de Lis.* Toronto: Hart & Company, 1890. p. 37. Print. ("Château Papineau" as quoted here is the first poem of a 5-villanelle sequence.)
5. Louis-Joseph Papineau (1786–1871) was the leader of the Rebellion of 1837–1838 in Lower Canada (*i.e.* Québec). He is a national hero.
6. Harrison, Susan Frances (writing as S. Frances Harrison). "Niagara in Winter." *Pine, Rose, and Fleur de Lis.* Toronto: Hart & Company, 1890. p. 196. Print. Also see: Gerson, Carole and Gwendolyn Davies, eds. *Canadian Poetry: From the Beginnings Through the First World War.* Toronto: McClelland & Stewart, 1994. p. 299. Print.
7. Harrison, Susan Frances (writing as S. Frances Harrison). "September." Rand, Theodore H., ed. *A Treasury of Canadian Verse.* London: J.M. Dent, 1900 and Toronto: William Briggs,

1900. p. 128. Print. Also see: Gerson, Carole and Gwendolyn Davies, eds. *Canadian Poetry: From the Beginnings Through the First World War*. Toronto: McClelland & Stewart, 1994. p. 298. Print.

Bliss Carman:
Poet of Transcendentalism

1. Rittenhouse, Jessie B. *The Younger American Poets*. First published in 1904. Reprinted in facsimile by Forgotten Books.
2. Untermeyer, Louis, ed. *Modern American Poetry: A Critical Anthology*. New York: Harcourt, Brace, 1919. Print. Reprinted in facsimile by Forgotten Books.
3. Both Carman and Emerson were descended from the 18th century lawyer and loyalist Daniel Bliss, of Concord, Massachusetts.
4. Emerson, Ralph Waldo. *Nature*. Boston: James Munroe and Company, 1836. Print. This essay is included in: Whicher, Stephen E., ed. *Selections from Ralph Waldo Emerson*. Boston: Houghton Mifflin, 1957. pp. 21–56. Print.
5. Emerson, Ralph Waldo. "Self-Reliance." *Essays: First Series*. 1841. Print. This essay is included in: Whicher, Stephen E., ed. *Selections from Ralph Waldo Emerson*. Boston: Houghton Mifflin, 1957. pp. 147–168. Print.
6. Whalen, Terry. *Bliss Carman and His Works*. Toronto: ECW Press, n.d. Print.
7. When Carole Gerson and Gwendolyn Davies compiled their important anthology, *Canadian Poetry: From the Beginnings Through the First World War*, they covered the field from Robert Hayman (1575–1629) through the close of the First World War. Canadian culture was different after the war because the trauma of this war divided the old Canada from the new Canada.
8. Delsartean unitrinianism: an æsthetic philosophy based on the work of François Alexandre Nicolas Chéri Delsarte (1811–1871).
9. It is not known if Dr. King was aware of his wife's intimacy with the young poet, or what he might have thought about it.

10. Carman would later write three poetry collections with Richard Hovey: *Songs From Vagabondia* (1894), *More Songs From Vagabondia* (1896), and *Last Songs From Vagabondia* (1901). These books were extremely popular.
11. Carman, Bliss, and Mary Perry King. *Daughters of Dawn: A Lyrical Pageant*. New York: Mitchell and Kennerley, 1913. Print. Carman, Bliss, and Mary Perry King. *Earth's Deities and other Rhythmic Masques*. New York: Mitchell and Kennerley, 1914. Print. These two books illustrate the commitment Carman and King had made to Delsartean theories.
12. Shepard, Odell. *Bliss Carman*. Toronto: McClelland & Stewart, 1923. p. 115. Print.
13. Carman, Bliss. *Low Tide on Grand Pré: A Book of Lyrics*. Cambridge & Chicago: Stone and Kimball, 1893. Print. "Low Tide on Grand Pré" (1887) along with its initial version, "Low Tide on Avon" (1886), are reprinted in: Gerson, Carole and Gwendolyn Davies, eds. *Canadian Poetry: From the Beginnings Through the First World War*. Toronto: McClelland & Stewart, 1994. pp. 230–231 and 227–229. Print.
14. Carman, Bliss and Richard Hovey. "A Vagabond Song." *More Songs from Vagabondia*. Boston: Copeland & Day, 1896. pp. 39–40. Print.
15. Quoted in: Shepard, Odell. *Bliss Carman*. Toronto: McClelland & Stewart, 1923. p. 118. Print.
16. Carman, Bliss. "The Winter Scene." *Sanctuary: Sunshine House Sonnets*. Toronto: McClelland & Stewart, 1929. Print.
17. Campbell, Wilfred, ed. *The Oxford Book of Canadian Verse*. Toronto: Oxford University Press, 1913. Print. In his "Preface," Campbell is clear that in 1913 he privileged verse that upheld the Christian values shared by most of the people living in English Canada: Canadians of English, Scots, or Irish ancestry. The following year, in the summer of 1914, a war broke out that would change all that forever.

Duncan Campbell Scott: *Poet of the Canadian Shield*

1. Ross, Malcolm, ed. *Poets of the Confederation*. Toronto: McClelland & Stewart, 1960. Print. See page 1 of his "Introduction."
2. Ross, Malcolm, ed. *Poets of the Confederation*. Toronto: McClelland & Stewart, 1960. Print. See page 2 of his "Introduction."
3. Treaty No. 9 (or the James Bay Treaty) was badly—some might say *fatally*—flawed. Duncan Campbell Scott realized this. However, he justified to himself his role in enacting this treaty with a belief that it was the best deal that could be achieved at the time, and with a hope that future Ontario and federal governments would act to correct the deficiencies, which were obvious from the start. They failed to do so, and much of the suffering experienced by the northern Cree and Ojibwa to this day—over a century later—is the result of Treaty No. 9. Perhaps because of events like this, Scott took to referring to the Indigenous People as a doomed race or a doomed nation.

As a Christian, Scott thought that winning North America for Christ could be part of God's plan for spreading the faith. (This was a common idea in those days.) Thus, he believed conversion was the only way for the Indigenous Peoples to survive. Events since 1905 have shown that he was wrong. Although a great deal of assimilation has occurred in the southern parts of Canada as Indigenous traditions were destroyed and people moved from the reserves into cities, this is not the entire story for First Nations located in the more remote and northern parts of the country. There are cases in the north where Indigenous languages and cultures have often been preserved and nurtured. Indigenous composer Jeremy Dutcher of the Tobique First Nation has declared,

"Canada, you are in the midst of an Indigenous renaissance." (*Reader's Digest* Vol. 194, No. 1,156 January/February 2019 p. 24.) And this renaissance is now obvious in all parts of the country. If the point of the program was to "solve the Indian problem," assimilation never worked; it was a terribly flawed concept. And at its base, assimilation reveals racist notions in the dominant group (in this case, White settlers) concerning those people to be assimilated.

4. The Truth and Reconciliation Commission of Canada. *Honouring the Truth, Reconciling for the Future: Summary of the Final Report of the Truth and Reconciliation Commission of Canada*. Winnipeg, 2015. p. 58.
5. An interesting commentary on Scott's relationship with the Indigenous People can be found in: Abley, Mark. *Conversations with a Dead Man: The Legacy of Duncan Campbell Scott*. Vancouver: Douglas & McIntyre, 2013. Print.
6. Campbell, Wilfred, ed. *The Oxford Book of Canadian Verse*. Toronto: Oxford University Press, 1913. Print. See the first page of Campbell's "Preface."
7. Purdy, Al. "The Country North of Belleville." *The Cariboo Horses*. Toronto: McClelland & Stewart, 1965. Print. The poem is also in *Beyond Remembering: The Collected Poems of Al Purdy*. Madeira Park, British Columbia: Harbour Publishing, 2000. pp. 79–81. Print.
8. Scott was a deeply religious man and he believed that all people should become Christians. This notion was in Scott's mind during the years he directed the infamous Residential School system, which was run by various Christian churches. In fact, it was during Scott's tenure that attendance at these schools became mandatory. This system proved to be disastrous. Although the function of these schools was to be "educational," in practice their goal was cultural genocide. As Prime Minister Stephen Harper famously put it in his apology in 2008, the goal was "to kill the Indian in the child." Unfortunately, cultural genocide at times became real

genocide. The tragic consequences of the Residential Schools, like those of Treaty No. 9, haunt Canada to the present day.

9. Duffy, Andrew. "The Battle for the Health of Indigenous Students." *Ottawa Citizen* 12 June 2021: A 8-9. Print. In this article, Andrew Duffy states that Duncan Campbell Scott prevented children in the Residential Schools from receiving proper health care, especially during the continual outbreaks of tuberculosis within the schools and in the Indigenous communities in general. This political conflict was between Dr. Peter Bryce, chief medical officer of the Departments of the Interior and Indian Affairs, and Scott. Dr. Bryce argued for increased medical treatment for the students in the Residential Schools; Scott disagreed. As a result, it is now thought that several thousand Indigenous children died, often from tuberculosis or pneumonia, as a result of the lack of proper medical care. It seems this travesty must be laid at Scott's feet.

(Also see: https://ottawacitizen.com/news/local-news/the-policy-battle-that-set-the-stage-for-a-century-of-residential-school-death-misery-grief)

It is well worth keeping in mind that Scott did not set up the Residential Schools. Scott served as the Deputy Superintendent of Indian Affairs from 1913 to 1932. The Residential Schools were established during the 1880s and lasted until 1996. This was a racist and brutal program Scott inherited from his predecessors. Long before Scott possessed any real authority at Indian Affairs, the racist attitudes behind these schools were well established; in fact, they were embedded in Canadian culture. In her article "Oh Canada, with not so Glowing Hearts, We See Thee Rise" (*First Monday* June 2021. Box 340, 395 Broadway Street, Wyoming, Ontario N0N 1T0) Amy Mayea quotes Prime Minister John A. Macdonald's position early on in the government's Residential Schools program: "Indian children should be withdrawn as much as possible from the parental influence, and the only way to do that would be to put them in central training industrial schools where they will acquire the habits and modes of thought of white men." In Macdonald's view this is because "When the school is on the reserve, the child lives with its parents, who are savages, and though he may learn to read and write, his habits and training mode of thought are Indian. He is simply a savage who can read and write." The idea that one could call the Indigenous People "savages" was, sadly, endemic in both Macdonald's day and in Scott's day. Of course, Scott must be responsible for what happened during his administration, such as refusing to provide necessary health care to First Nations People.

It would be a shame, and a loss for Canadian literature, if the recent discovery of thousands of unmarked and unrecorded graves of Indigenous children were permitted to obscure the value and quality of Scott's poetry. Whatever Scott did or did not do as a federal civil servant (his record certainly does not look good) he remains among Canada's most important poets. And he certainly forms a crucial bridge from the Confederation Period to our poets of the Modern Period like Dorothy Livesay, Al Purdy, and Raymond Souster.

10. In an article published in 1947 (the year Scott died), E.K. Brown advanced the theory that the North is the home of the Ontarian's imagination. See: Brown, E.K. "Now, Take Ontario." *Maclean's Magazine* 15 June 1947. Print. Certainly Duncan Campbell Scott would agree with this.
11. Johnston, Gordon. *Duncan Campbell Scott and His Works*. Toronto: ECW Press, n.d. Print.
12. The Group of Seven—Franklin Carmichael, Lawren Harris, A.Y. Jackson, Frank Johnston, Arthur Lismer, J.E.H. MacDonald, and Frederick Varley—was founded in 1920. They are the visual arts equivalent of the Confederation Poets.
13. In *Duncan Campbell Scott and His Works*, Gordon Johnston put it this way: "The spell which then overtakes him is the actual experience of transcendence, and it seems to him 'deeper than peace.'"
14. Scott, Duncan Campbell. "The Height of Land." *Lundy's Lane and Other Poems*. New York: George H. Doran Company, 1916. Print. Facsimile edition by Forgotten Books. pp. 68–76.

15. *ibid.* pp. 68–69.
16. *ibid.* pp. 70–71.
17. *ibid.* p. 72.

"The Height of Land," one of Scott's most important poems, can also be found in:

Gerson, Carole and Gwendolyn Davies, eds. *Canadian Poetry: From the Beginnings Through the First World War.* Toronto: McClelland & Stewart, 1994. pp. 277–281. Print.

and Ross, Malcolm, ed. *Poets of the Confederation.* Toronto: McClelland & Stewart, 1960. pp. 109–112. Print.

18. Scott, Duncan Campbell. "On the Way to the Mission." *New World Lyrics and Ballads.* Toronto: George N. Morang, 1905. Print.
19. Scott, Duncan Campbell. "The Half-Breed Girl." *Via Borealis.* Toronto: Tyrell, 1906. Print.
20. Scott, Duncan Campbell. "The Onondaga Madonna." *Labour and the Angel.* Boston: Copeland & Day, 1898. p. 15. Print.
21. Scott, Duncan Campbell. "The Forsaken." *New World Lyrics and Ballads.* Toronto: George N. Morang, 1905. Print.
22. Johnston, Gordon. *Duncan Campbell Scott and His Works.* Toronto: ECW Press, n.d. Print.

E. Pauline Johnson [Tekahionwake]: *Poet of the Mohawk People*

1. Johnson, E. Pauline. *Flint and Feather.* (The complete poems of E. Pauline Johnson.) Toronto: The Musson Book Co., 1912. Print. Reprinted by PaperJacks in 1972. Print. This single volume contains all of Johnson's poems from *The White Wampum* and *Canadian Born* plus twenty Miscellaneous Poems, previously uncollected.
2. Atwood, Margaret, ed. *The New Oxford Book of Canadian Verse in English.* Toronto: Oxford University Press, 1982. Print. Atwood selected "Ojistoh" and "Marshlands."
3. Due to renewed interest in Canada's Indigenous Peoples, there has been much fresh reading of writers such as E. Pauline Johnson. Two interesting books published this century are:

Strong-Boag, Veronica and Carole Gerson. *Paddling Her Own Canoe: Times and Texts of E. Pauline Johnson (Tekahionwake).* Toronto: University of Toronto Press, 2000. Print.

Gerson, Carole and Veronica Strong-Boag, eds. *E. Pauline Johnson, Tekahionwake: Collected Poems and Selected Prose.* Toronto: University of Toronto Press, 2002. Print.

4. Johnson, E. Pauline. *The White Wampum.* London: The Bodley Head, 1895. Print.
5. Johnson, E. Pauline. *Canadian Born.* Toronto: George N. Morang, 1903. Print.
6. Johnson, E. Pauline. *Legends of Vancouver.* Vancouver: Privately printed, 1911. Print.
7. Johnson, E. Pauline. *The Moccasin Maker.* Toronto: William Briggs, 1913. Print.

8. Johnson, E. Pauline. *The Shagganappi*. Toronto: William Briggs, 1913. Print.
9. Johnson, E. Pauline. "Erie Waters." *The White Wampum*. London: The Bodley Head, 1895. Print.
10. Johnson, E. Pauline. "Marshlands." *The White Wampum*. London: The Bodley Head, 1895. Print.
11. Johnson, E. Pauline. "The Pilot of the Plains." *The White Wampum*. London: The Bodley Head, 1895. Print.
12. Johnson, E. Pauline. "As Red Men Die." *The White Wampum*. London: The Bodley Head, 1895. Print.
13. Johnson, E. Pauline. "The Corn Husker." *Canadian Born*. Toronto: George N. Morang, 1903. Print.
14. Johnson, E. Pauline. "Canadian Born." *Canadian Born*. Toronto: George N. Morang, 1903. Print.
15. Johnson, E. Pauline. "Under Canvas." *The White Wampum*. London: The Bodley Head, 1895. Print.
16. Johnson, E. Pauline. "The Song My Paddle Sings." *The White Wampum*. London: The Bodley Head, 1895. Print. Well over a century later, this continues to be Johnson's most popular poem.
17. Johnson, E. Pauline. "And He Said, Fight On." *Flint and Feather*. Don Mills (Toronto): PaperJacks/General Publishing, 1972. p. 164. Print. It was written on Johnson's deathbed.

Ethelwyn Wetherald: *Poet of the Eramosa*

1. Wetherald, Ethelwyn. *Tree-Top Mornings*. Boston: Cornhill, 1921. Print.
2. Wetherald, Ethelwyn. "Hester Prynne Speaks." *Lyrics and Sonnets*. Toronto, Nelson, 1931. Print. Collected along with six other of her poems in: Gerson, Carole and Gwendolyn Davies, eds. *Canadian Poetry: From the Beginnings Through the First World War*. Toronto: McClelland & Stewart, 1994. p. 317. Print.
3. Hawthorne, Nathaniel. *The Scarlet Letter: A Romance*. Boston: Ticknor, Reed, and Fields, 1850. Print.
4. Wetherald, Ethelwyn. "The Screech-Owl." *The Last Robin: Lyrics and Sonnets*. Toronto: William Briggs, 1907. p. 10. Print. Also collected in: Garvin, John W., ed. *Canadian Poets*. Toronto: McClelland, Goodchild & Stewart, Publishers, 1916. p. 169. Print.
5. Gordon, Katherine L. "An Appreciation For Agnes Ethelwyn Wetherald." This unpublished piece was sent to the author on 4 March 2017.
6. Campbell so valued her work that he included eight of her poems in *The Oxford Book of Canadian Verse*. Toronto: Oxford University Press, 1913. Print.
7. Wetherald, Ethelwyn. "A Winter Picture." *Tangled in Stars*. Boston: Richard G. Badger, 1902. Print. Collected along with six other of her poems in: Gerson, Carole and Gwendolyn Davies, eds. *Canadian Poetry: From the Beginnings Through the First World War*. Toronto: McClelland & Stewart, 1994. p. 316. Print.
8. Wetherald, Ethelwyn. "To February." Rand, Theodore H., ed. *A Treasury of Canadian Verse*. London: J.M. Dent, 1900 and Toronto: William Briggs, 1900. pp. 377–378. Print.

9. Wetherald, Ethelwyn. “Moonlight.” *The House of the Trees, and Other Poems*. Boston: Lamson, Wolffe, 1895. Print.
10. Garvin, J.W., ed. *The Collected Poems of Isabella Valancy Crawford*. Toronto: William Briggs, 1905. See the “Introduction” by Ethelwyn Wetherald, pp. 15–29. Print.
11. Wetherald, Ethelwyn. “Youth and Age.” *The Last Robin: Lyrics and Sonnets*. Toronto: William Briggs, 1907. p. 36. Print.

Helena Coleman:
Poet of the First World War

1. Coleman, Helena. "On the Trail." *Songs and Sonnets*. Toronto: The Tennyson Club of Toronto/William Briggs, 1906. pp. 29–31. Print. Also collected in: Campbell, Wilfred, ed. *The Oxford Book of Canadian Verse*. Toronto: Oxford University Press, 1913. pp. 285–286. Print.
2. Coleman, Helena. "Indian Summer." *Songs and Sonnets*. Toronto: The Tennyson Club of Toronto/William Briggs, 1906. pp. 13–15. Print.
3. Coleman, Helena. "Among the Mountains." *Songs and Sonnets*. Toronto: The Tennyson Club of Toronto/William Briggs, 1906. p. 117. Print.
4. Coleman, Helena. "Vanished Years." *Songs and Sonnets*. Toronto: The Tennyson Club of Toronto/William Briggs, 1906. p. 154. Print.
5. Coleman, Helena. "When First He Put the Khaki On." *Marching Men: War Verses*. Toronto: J.M. Dent, 1917. p. 13. Print. Collected along with two other of her poems in: Gerson, Carole and Gwendolyn Davies, eds. *Canadian Poetry: From the Beginnings Through the First World War*. Toronto: McClelland & Stewart, 1994. pp. 360–361. Print.
6. Coleman, Helena. *Songs*. Toronto: Ryerson Press, 1937. Print. "On the Trail" and "Among the Mountains" are included.
7. Although seven of our poets—Sir Charles G.D. Roberts, Frederick George Scott, William Douw Lighthall, Sophia M. Almon Hensley, Duncan Campbell Scott, Ethelwyn Wetherald, and Helena Coleman—survived both the First World War and the Great Depression, living long lives into the 1940s and 1950s, only Roberts in 1941 and D.C. Scott in 1947 would publish later than

Coleman's *Songs* in 1937. Modern Canada was not a congenial environment for these former Victorians, and their poetry was no longer congenial to modern tastes that were more in tune with the poetry of Irving Layton and Al Purdy. As good as these Confederation Poets were, CanLit had passed them by.

Conclusion

1. Another, and perhaps more useful, way to look at the Confederation Period is to take the date of Sir Charles G.D. Roberts' *Orion* (1880) as the first volume by a Confederation Poet and the publication of the final poetry collection by Roberts, *Canada Speaks of Britain and Other Poems of the War* (1941), as the boundaries. In this way, Roberts opens and closes the period. But however neat that might seem, the First World War changed Canada. After 1920, the old Canada was vanishing, much as the old Britain was also vanishing. Therefore, the Confederation Period, properly considered, will be 1880 to the conclusion of the First World War. No matter how one wants to consider the Confederation Period, Sir Charles G.D. Roberts was the Father of Canadian Literature.
2. Canada's Indigenous Peoples, as important as they were in 1867—and continue to be today—were left out of Confederation. And so were women. The Fathers of Confederation were *fathers* because when the meetings were held to create Canada, neither women nor Indigenous people were "persons" under the laws of the day. Limiting the Confederation process to White men was a grave error.

I wish to make one more observation. In the past the editors of anthologies and the authors of textbooks (*i.e.,* the keepers of the CanLit canon) have almost exclusively been men. (Of the fifteen anthology editors mentioned in this book, only three—that is merely 20%—are women, Margaret Atwood among them.) As one might expect, the bulk of the poems from the Confederation Period included in these anthologies and textbooks have been by male poets. Yet, six of our Confederation poets are women; that's

40% of the poets publishing during their era. Perhaps even more surprising, of the six women covered here, two of them—Sophia M. Almon Hensley and Helena Coleman—have no entry in *The Oxford Companion to Canadian Literature*. And only two of the six—Isabella Valancy Crawford and E. Pauline Johnson—have poetry included by Margaret Atwood in her 1982 edition of *The New Oxford Book of Canadian Verse in English*. One might assume that the poetry of our Confederation Era women fails to meet the elevated criteria used by the keepers of the canon. However, an actual reading of the books by these women reveals a great many fine poems of lasting merit. Still, these women and their poetry have been, and continue to be, largely overlooked. The same has too often been true of the female writers of fiction. I would like to see the poetry and fiction of Confederation Era women reconsidered by the makers of school anthologies and textbooks.

The same holds true for Indigenous writers. They have been ignored by the literary establishment as much or more than our women have been shunted aside. Their underrepresentation has gone on far too long. In fact, the discrimination against First Nations and other non-White writers is so persistent in the literary arts that despite Afro-Métis writer George Elliott Clarke serving as Canada's Parliamentary Poet Laureate when I began to write this book, and the current Parliamentary Poet Laureate being the Cree poet Sky Dancer as I finish my work, Indigenous, Black, and Asian literary people founded the BIPOC of Publishing, a not-for-profit collective, in 2019. That a hundred and fifty-two years after Confederation racism is still so prominent in CanLit circles that there is a need for a BIPOC Collective is a national shame. (Reported in the Summer 2021 issue of *Write*.) The history of Indigenous poetry from Ojibwa writer Kah-Ge-Ga-Gah-Bowh in the 1840s and 1850s (today he is recognized as a "National Historic Person" in Canada) to Cree poet Sky Dancer has been obscured by generations of neglect.

Epilogue: *Confederation Poetry in the Postmodern Era*

1. Lampman, Archibald. "In November." *Among the Millet, and Other Poems.* Ottawa: J. Durie and Son, 1888. p. 144. Print. Also included in: Souster, Raymond, ed. *Comfort of the Fields.* Sutton West, Ontario: The Paget Press, 1979. p. 83. Print.
2. Lampman, Archibald. "In November." *Lyrics of Earth.* Boston: Copeland & Day, 1895. pp. 40–42. Print. Also included in: Souster, Raymond, ed. *Comfort of the Fields.* Sutton West, Ontario: The Paget Press, 1979. pp. 81–82. Print.
3. Meyer, Bruce. Letter to the author. 11 May 2020, in which Meyer states: "Then there's Archibald Lampman's 'In November,' a poem I consider the first modern Canadian poem. I recall reading that and the poem had a big impact on me."
4. Lampman, Archibald. *Alcyone, and Other Poems.* Ottawa: James Ogilvy, 1899. Print.
5. Lampman, Archibald. "We Too Shall Sleep." *Alcyone, and Other Poems.* Ottawa: James Ogilvy, 1899. Print.
6. Bowering, George. Letter to the author. 8 May 2020. Bowering's letter contained a brief essay, "Archibald Lampman: 'We Too Shall Sleep.'"
7. Briesmaster, Allan. Letter to the author. 9 May 2020. Briesmaster's letter contained his two tribute poems. Both tribute poems are included in: Briesmaster, Allan. *Interstellar.* Toronto: Quattro Books, 2007. Print. And "Winter Night, Looking North" is also included in: Briesmaster, Allan. *The Long Bond: Selected and New Poems.* Toronto: Guernica Editions, 2019. p. 60. Print.
8. Moritz, A.F. Letter to the author. 11 May 2020. After commenting on Lampman's influence on his own poetry, Moritz

ruefully adds, "I think of Lampman as a poet who always should be—but never is—on any list of the truly fine English-language poets of the 1890s ..."

9. Lee, John B. Letter to the author. 8 May 2020. Lee observes that "Archibald Lampman figured large in my youth. We passed through Morpeth on our way to the lake either cycling with my sister or my friends, or driving by car. My great grandfather Woofenden was a blacksmith in Morpeth. My great aunt Em Lee had a cottage at Rondeau. I often passed the cairn on number 3 highway west of Morpeth where there is a cairn dedicated to the memory of Lampman."
10. Inman, Keith. Letter to the author. 9 May 2020. Inman's letter contained his brief essay, "I Sometimes Stop By Archie's Place."
11. Clarke, George Elliott. Letter to the author. 8 May 2020.
12. Morton, Colin. Letter to the author. 8 May 2020.
13. Wayman, Tom. Letter to the author. 8 May 2020. Wayman's letter contained his essay "My Confederation Poets."
14. Clarke, George Elliott. Letter to the author. 8 May 2020.
15. Mutala, Marion. Letter to the author. 12 May 2020. Mutala's letter contained her brief essay "Confederation Poets."
16. Wolff, Elana. Letter to the author. 12 May 2020. Wolff's letter contained her essay "Pauline Johnson, the Imprints."
17. Shenfeld, Karen. Letter to the author. 12 May 2020. Included in Shenfeld's letter was her tribute poem to Pauline Johnson, "Canoeing Song."
18. Wayman, Tom. Letter to the author. 8 May 2020. Wayman's letter contained his essay "My Confederation Poets."
19. Alexander, Becky D. Letter to the author. 10 May 2020.
20. Marchand, Blaine. Letter to the author. 8 May 2020.
21. Rogers, Linda. Letter to the author. 9 May 2020. Rogers' letter contained her essay "Genetic Recognition and the Eve Blanket."
22. Carman, Bliss. "Low Tide on Grand Pré." *Low Tide on Grand Pré: A Book of Lyrics*. Cambridge & Chicago: Stone and Kimball, 1893. pp. 15–18. Print.

23. Eaton, Margaret Patricia. Letter to the author. 8 May 2020, first letter.
24. Eaton, Margaret Patricia. Letter to the author. 8 May 2020, second letter.
25. Eaton, Margaret Patricia. Letter to the author. 8 May 2020, second letter.
26. Gervais, Marty. Letter to the author. 10 May 2020.
27. Clarke, George Elliott. Letter to the author. 8 May 2020.
28. Eaton, Margaret Patricia. Letter to the author. 8 May 2020, first letter.
29. These initial poetry collections are: Sir Charles G.D. Roberts: *Orion, and Other Poems* (Philadelphia: J.B. Lippincott & Co., 1880); Barry Straton: *Lays of Love, and Miscellaneous Poems* (Saint John, New Brunswick: J. & A. McMillan, 1884); Sophie Almon Hensley: *Poems* (Windsor, Nova Scotia: J.J. Anslow, 1889); John Frederic Herbin: *Canada, and Other Poems* (Windsor, Nova Scotia: J.J. Anslow, 1891); Bliss Carman: *Low Tide on Grand Pré: A Book of Lyrics* (Cambridge & Chicago: Stone and Kimball, 1893).

During this same thirteen-year period, eight other Confederation Poets saw their first poetry collections published: Isabella Valancy Crawford, Frederick George Scott, George Frederick Cameron, William Douw Lighthall, Archibald Lampman, Wilfred Campbell, Susan Frances Harrison, and Duncan Campbell Scott.

30. Klinck, C.F. and R.E. Watters, eds. *Canadian Anthology.* Toronto: W.J. Gage, 1955. pp. 142–143. Print.
31. David, Jack and Robert Lecker, eds. *Canadian Poetry, Volume One.* Toronto: General Publishing, 1982. pp. 288–290. Print.
32. Mezei, Kathy. "D.C. Scott." David, Jack and Robert Lecker, eds. *Canadian Poetry, Volume One.* Toronto: General Publishing, 1982. p. 289. Print.
33. Abley, Mark. *Conversations with a Dead Man: The Legacy of Duncan Campbell Scott.* Vancouver: Douglas & McIntyre, 2013. Print.
34. Scott, Duncan Campbell. "Autumn Song." *Labour and the Angel.* Boston: Copeland & Day, 1898. Print. Also in: Campbell, Wilfred,

ed. *The Oxford Book of Canadian Verse*. Toronto: Oxford University Press, 1913. pp. 223–224. Print.

35. Sky Dancer won the Milton Acorn Memorial People's Poetry Award for her first poetry collection, *Bear Bones & Feathers* (Coteau Books, 1994). Since then she has been a major voice in Canadian poetry.

Selected Bibliography

Primary Sources: Works by the Poets Studied

Cameron, George Frederick. *Lyrics on Freedom, Love and Death.* Cameron, Charles J., ed. Printed by the *Daily News*, Kingston, Ontario, 1887. Print.

Campbell, Wilfred. *The Beauty, History, Romance and Mystery of the Canadian Lake Region.* Toronto: The Musson Book Co., 1910. Print.

—. *Beyond the Hills of Dream.* Boston: Houghton Mifflin, 1899. Print.

—. *The Dread Voyage Poems.* Toronto: William Briggs, 1893. Print.

—. *Lake Lyrics and Other Poems.* Saint John, New Brunswick: J. & A. McMillan, 1889. Print.

—. *Sagas of Vaster Britain: Poems of the Race, the Empire and the Divinity of Man.* Toronto: The Musson Book Co., 1914. Print.

—. *Snowflakes and Sunbeams.* St. Stephen, New Brunswick: *The Saint Croix Courier* Press, 1888. Print.

—. *Vapour and Blue: Souster selects Campbell: the poetry of William Wilfred Campbell.* Souster, Raymond, ed. Sutton West, Ontario: The Paget Press, 1978. Print.

Campbell, Wilfred, Archibald Lampman, Duncan Campbell Scott. *At The Mermaid Inn: Wilfred Campbell, Archibald Lampman, Duncan Campbell Scott in* The Globe *1892-3.* Toronto: University of Toronto Press, 1979. Print.

Campbell, Wilfred, ed. *The Oxford Book of Canadian Verse.* Toronto: Oxford University Press, 1913. Print. Facsimile edition, with a new "Introduction" by Len Early, published by OUP in 2013. Print.

Carman, Bliss. *Low Tide on Grand Pré: A Book of Lyrics.* Cambridge & Chicago: Stone and Kimball, 1893. Print.

—. *Sanctuary: Sunshine House Sonnets.* Toronto: McClelland & Stewart, 1929. Print.

—. *Windflower: Poems of Bliss Carman*. Souster, Raymond and Douglas Lochhead, eds. Ottawa: Tecumseh Press, 1985. Print.

Carman, Bliss and Richard Hovey. *Last Songs from Vagabondia*. Boston: Small, Maynard, 1901. Print.

—. *More Songs from Vagabondia*. Boston: Copeland & Day, 1896. Print.

—. *Songs from Vagabondia*. Boston: Copeland & Day, 1894. Print.

Carman, Bliss, and Mary Perry King. *Daughters of Dawn: A Lyrical Pageant*. New York: Mitchell and Kennerley, 1913. Print.

—. *Earth's Deities and other Rhythmic Masques*. New York: Mitchell and Kennerley, 1914. Print.

Coleman, Helena. *Marching Men: War Verses*. Toronto: J.M. Dent, 1917. Print.

—. *Songs: A Selection of Earlier Sonnets and Lyrics*. Toronto: Ryerson Press, 1937. Print. Facsimile edition by Forgotten Books (FB &c Ltd., Dalton House, 60 Windsor Avenue, London SW19 2RR, England). Print.

—. *Songs and Sonnets*. Toronto: The Tennyson Club of Toronto/William Briggs, 1906. Print.

Crawford, Isabella Valancy. *The Collected Poems of Isabella Valancy Crawford*. Garvin, J.W., ed. Toronto: William Briggs, 1905. Print. Facsimile edition, with a new "Introduction" by James Reaney, published as *Collected Poems*. Toronto: University of Toronto Press, 1972. Print.

—. *Fairy Tales of Isabella Valancy Crawford*. Petrone, Penny, ed. Ottawa: Borealis Press, 1977. Print.

—. *Old Spookses' Pass, Malcolm's Katie and Other Poems*. Toronto: James Bain and Son, 1884. Print.

—. *Selected Stories of Isabella Valancy Crawford*. Petrone, Penny, ed. Ottawa: University of Ottawa Press, 1975. Print.

Harrison, Susan Frances. *Crowded Out! And Other Sketches*. Ottawa: *The Evening Journal*, 1886. Print.

—. (writing as S. Frances Harrison). *Later Poems And New Villanelles*. Toronto: Ryerson Press, 1928. Print.

—. (writing as S. Frances Harrison). *Pine, Rose, and Fleur de Lis*. Toronto: Hart & Company, 1890. Print.

Hensley, Sophia M. Almon (writing as Almon Hensley). *The Heart of a Woman*. New York: G.P. Putnam's Sons, 1906. Print.

—. (writing as Sophie M. Almon). *Poems*. Windsor, Nova Scotia: J.J. Anslow, 1889. Print.

—. (writing as Sophie M. Almon-Hensley). *A Woman's Love Letters*. New York: J. Selwyn Tait and Sons, 1895. Print.

Herbin, John Frederic. *Canada, and Other Poems*. Windsor, Nova Scotia: J.J. Anslow, 1891. Print.

—. *The Marshlands: Souvenir in Song of the Land of Evangeline*. Windsor, Nova Scotia: J.J. Anslow, 1893. Print.

—. *The Marshlands and The Trail of the Tide*. Toronto: William Briggs, 1899. Print. Facsimile edition by Franklin Classics. Print.

Johnson, E. Pauline. *Canadian Born*. Toronto: George N. Morang, 1903. Print.

—. *E. Pauline Johnson, Tekahionwake: Collected Poems and Selected Prose*. Gerson, Carole and Veronica Strong-Boag, eds. Toronto: University of Toronto Press, 2002. Print.

—. *Flint and Feather*. Toronto: The Musson Book Co., 1912. Print. Reprinted by PaperJacks in 1972. Print.

—. *Legends of Vancouver*. Vancouver: Privately printed, 1911. Print.

—. *The Moccasin Maker*. Toronto: William Briggs, 1913. Print.

—. *The Shagganappi*. Toronto: William Briggs, 1913. Print.

—. *The White Wampum*. London: The Bodley Head, 1895. Print.

Lampman, Archibald. *Alcyone, and Other Poems*. Ottawa: James Ogilvy, 1899. Print.

—. *Among the Millet, and Other Poems*. Ottawa: J. Durie and Son, 1888. Print.

—. *Archibald Lampman: Selected Prose*. Davies, Barrie, ed. Ottawa: Tecumseh Press, 1975. Print.

—. *At the Long Sault, and Other New Poems*. Scott, Duncan Campbell, ed. Toronto: Ryerson Press, 1943. Print.

—. *Comfort of the Fields: Archibald Lampman, The best-known Poems*. Souster, Raymond, ed. Sutton West, Ontario: The Paget Press, 1979. Print.

—. *Lampman's Kate: Late Love Poems of Archibald Lampman, 1887–1897*. Whitridge, Margaret Coulby, ed. Ottawa: Borealis Press, 1975. Print.

—. *Lyrics of Earth*. Boston: Copeland & Day, 1895. Print.

—. *The Poems of Archibald Lampman*. Scott, Duncan Campbell, ed. Toronto: George N. Morang, 1900. Print.

Lighthall, William Douw (writing as W.D. Lighthall). *Old Measures: Collected Verse*. Montreal: A.T. Chapman, 1922 and Toronto: The Musson Book Co., 1922. Print.

—. *Thoughts, Moods and Ideals: Crimes of Leisure*. Montreal: "Witness" Printing House, 1887. Print.

Lighthall, William Douw, ed. *Songs of the Great Dominion: Voices from the Forests and Waters, the Settlements and Cities of Canada*. London: Walter Scott, "Windsor Series," 1889. Print.

Roberts, Charles G.D. *The Book of the Native*. Toronto: Copp Clark, 1896. Print.

—. *Canada Speaks of Britain and Other Poems of the War*. Toronto: Ryerson Press, 1941. Print.

—. *The Iceberg and Other Poems*. Toronto: Ryerson Press, 1934. Print.

—. *In Divers Tones*. Boston: D. Lothrop and Company, 1886. Print.

—. *New Poems*. London: Constable, 1919. Print.

—. *New York Nocturnes, and Other Poems*. Boston: Lamson, Wolffe, 1898. Print.

—. *Orion, and Other Poems*. Philadelphia: J.B. Lippincott & Co., 1880. Print.

—. *The Selected Poems of Sir Charles G.D. Roberts*. Pacey, Desmond, ed. Toronto: Ryerson Press, 1955. Print.

—. *Songs of the Common Day and Ave!: An Ode for the Shelley Centenary*. London and New York: Longmans, Green, and Co., 1893. Print. Facsimile edition by Bibliolife (Bibliolife, P.O. Box 21206, Charleston, South Carolina, 29413, U.S.A.). Print.

Sangster, Charles. *Norland Echoes and Other Strains and Lyrics*. Tierney, Frank M., ed. Ottawa: Tecumseh Press, 1976. Print.

—. *The St. Lawrence and the Saguenay, and Other Poems*. Kingston, C.W. [Canada West]: John Creighton and John Duff, 1856 and New York: Miller, Orton & Mulligan, 1856. Print.

—. *The St. Lawrence and the Saguenay, and Other Poems* (Revised

Edition). Tierney, Frank M., ed. Ottawa: Tecumseh Press, 1984. Print.

Scott, Duncan Campbell. *Labour and the Angel.* Boston: Copeland & Day, 1898. Print.

—. *Lundy's Lane, and Other Poems.* New York: George H. Doran Company, 1916. Print. Facsimile edition by Forgotten Books (FB &c Ltd., Dalton House, 60 Windsor Avenue, London SW19 2RR, England). Print.

—. *The Magic House, and Other Poems.* London: Methuen, 1893. Print.

—. *New World Lyrics and Ballads.* Toronto: George N. Morang, 1905. Print.

—. *Powassan's Drum: Poems of Duncan Campbell Scott.* Souster, Raymond and Douglas Lochhead, eds. Ottawa: Tecumseh Press, 1985. Print.

—. *Via Borealis.* Toronto: Tyrell, 1906. Print.

Scott, Frederick George. *Collected Poems.* Vancouver: Clarke & Stuart, 1934. Print.

—. *The Great War As I Saw It.* Toronto: F.D. Goodchild, 1922. Print.

—. *Poems Old and New.* London: Society for Promoting Christian Knowledge, 1936. Print.

—. *The Soul's Quest, and Other Poems.* London: Kegan Paul, Trench, 1888. Print.

—. *The Unnamed Lake, and Other Poems.* Toronto: William Briggs, 1897. Print.

Straton, Barry. *Lays of Love, and Miscellaneous Poems.* Saint John, New Brunswick: J. & A. McMillan, 1884. Print.

Wetherald, Ethelwyn. *The House of the Trees, and Other Poems.* Boston: Lamson, Wolffe, 1895. Print.

—. *The Last Robin: Lyrics and Sonnets.* Toronto: William Briggs, 1907. Print.

—. *Lyrics and Sonnets.* Toronto: Nelson, 1931. Print.

—. *Tangled in Stars.* Boston: Richard G. Badger, 1902. Print.

—. *Tree-Top Mornings.* Boston: Cornhill, 1921. Print.

Major Anthologies containing Works by the Confederation Poets

Atwood, Margaret, ed. *The New Oxford Book of Canadian Verse in English.* Toronto: Oxford University Press, 1982. Print.

Burpee, Lawrence J., ed. *A Century of Canadian Sonnets.* Toronto: The Musson Book Co., 1910. Print.

Campbell, Wilfred, ed. *The Oxford Book of Canadian Verse.* Toronto: Oxford University Press, 1913. Print. Facsimile edition, with a new "Introduction" by Len Early, published by OUP in 2013. Print.

David, Jack and Robert Lecker, eds. *Canadian Poetry, Volume One.* Toronto: General Publishing, 1982. Print.

Garvin, John W., ed. *Canadian Poets.* Toronto: McClelland, Goodchild & Stewart, 1916. Print.

Gerson, Carole and Gwendolyn Davies, eds. *Canadian Poetry: From the Beginnings Through the First World War.* Toronto: McClelland & Stewart, 1994. Print.

Klinck, C.F. and R.E. Watters, eds. *Canadian Anthology.* Toronto: W.J. Gage, 1955. Print.

Lighthall, William Douw, ed. *Songs of the Great Dominion: Voices from the Forests and Waters, the Settlements and Cities of Canada.* London: Walter Scott, "Windsor Series," 1889. Print.

Lochhead, Douglas and Raymond Souster, eds. *100 Poems of Nineteenth Century Canada.* Toronto: Macmillan of Canada, 1974. Print.

Rand, Theodore H., ed. *A Treasury of Canadian Verse.* London: J.M. Dent, 1900 and Toronto: William Briggs, 1900. Print.

Ross, Malcolm, ed. *Poets of the Confederation.* Toronto: McClelland and Stewart, 1960. Print.

Secondary Sources: Other Works Consulted / Cited

Abbot Anthony. Quoted in: Merton, Thomas, trans. *The Wisdom of the Desert.* New York: New Directions, 1960. Print.

Abley, Mark. *Conversations with a Dead Man: The Legacy of Duncan Campbell Scott*. Vancouver: Douglas & McIntyre, 2013. Print.

Acorn, Milton. *Jackpine Sonnets*. Toronto: Steel Rail Educational Publishing, 1977. Print.

Alt, Marlene. "Charles Sangster." *The Canadian Encyclopedia*. Edmonton: Hurtig Publishers, 1985. Print.

Arnason, David, ed. *Isolation in Canadian Literature*. Toronto: Macmillan of Canada, 1975. Print.

Barker, Terry. "Charles Sangster and the True North." *Canadian Stories* 24.142 (2021-2022) pp. 56–70. Print.

—. *Tracing the True North: Two Essays*. Mississauga, Ontario: SureWay Press, 2021. Print.

—. "Tracking the True North." *Canadian Stories* 22.126 (2019) pp. 64–66. Print.

Brown, E.K. "Now, Take Ontario." *Maclean's Magazine* 15 June 1947. Print.

—. *On Canadian Poetry*. Toronto: McGraw-Hill Ryerson, 1943. Print. Reprinted in 1973 by the Tecumseh Press. Print.

—. *Responses and Evaluations: Essays On Canada*. Toronto: McClelland & Stewart, 1977. Print.

Bulfinch, Thomas. *Mythology*. New York: Dell Publishing, 1959. Print.

Burns, Robert Alan. *Isabella Valancy Crawford and Her Works*. Toronto: ECW Press, n.d. Print.

Christian, William and Colin Campbell. *Political Parties and Ideologies in Canada: Liberals, Conservatives, Socialists, Nationalists*. Toronto: McGraw-Hill Ryerson, 3rd edition, 1990. Print.

Cogswell, Fred. *Charles G.D. Roberts and His Works*. Toronto: ECW Press, n.d. Print.

Conway, Don. "Charles Sangster." *Canadian Poetry, Volume One*. Toronto: General Publishing, 1982. Print.

Davies, Barrie, ed. *At the Mermaid Inn: Wilfred Campbell, Archibald Lampman, Duncan Campbell Scott in* The Globe *1892-3*. Toronto: University of Toronto Press, 1979. Print.

Dewart, Edward Hartley, ed. *Selections from Canadian Poets*. Montreal: J. Lovell, 1864. Print. Reprinted by the University of Toronto Press in 1972. Print.

Dictionary of Canadian Biography. Toronto and Québec: University of Toronto and Université Laval, 1966.

Duffy, Andrew. "The Battle for the Health of Indigenous Students." *Ottawa Citizen* 12 June 2021: A 8-9. Print.

Early, L.R. *Archibald Lampman and His Works*. Toronto: ECW Press, n.d. Print.

Emerson, Ralph Waldo. *Essays: First Series*. 1841. Print.

—. *Nature*. Boston: James Munroe and Company, 1836. Print.

—. *Selections from Ralph Waldo Emerson*. Whicher, Stephen E., ed. Boston: Houghton Mifflin, 1957. Print.

Frye, Northrop. *The Bush Garden: Essays on the Canadian Imagination*. Toronto: House of Anansi, 1971. Print.

Galvin, Elizabeth McNeill. *Isabella Valancy Crawford: We Scarcely Knew Her*. Toronto: Natural Heritage/Natural History, 1994. Print.

Gaspar, Doris, Eleanor Gignac, Terrance Hamilton Hall, William Jarvis, Jennifer MacLeod, Olga Semeniuk, and Mike White, eds. *Amherstburg 1796-1996: The New Town on the Garrison Grounds*. Amherstburg, Ontario: Amherstburg Bicentennial Book Committee, 1996. Print.

Gayley, Charles Mills, C.C. Young, and Benjamin Putnam Kurtz, eds. *English Poetry: Its Principles and Progress*. New York: The Macmillan Company, 1920. Print.

Gnarowski, Michael, ed. *Archibald Lampman*. Toronto: Ryerson Press (Critical Views on Canadian Writers Series), 1970. Print.

Grant, George. *Lament for a Nation: The Defeat of Canadian Nationalism*. Toronto: McClelland and Stewart, 1965. Print.

Hawthorne, Nathaniel. *The Scarlet Letter: A Romance*. Boston: Ticknor, Reed, and Fields, 1850. Print.

Heavysege, Charles. *Sonnets*. Montreal: H. & G.M. Rose, 1855. Print.

Horsman, Reginald. *Matthew Elliott, British Indian Agent*. Detroit: Wayne State University Press, 1964. Print.

Johnson, Donald S. *Charting the Sea of Darkness*. New York: TAB Books, McGraw-Hill, 1993. Print.

Johnston, Gordon. *Duncan Campbell Scott and His Works*. Toronto: ECW Press, n.d. Print.

Keats, John. "Ode on a Grecian Urn." My copy-text is: Gayley, Charles Mills, C.C. Young, and Benjamin Putnam Kurtz, eds. *English Poetry: Its Principles and Progress.* New York: The Macmillan Company, 1920. Print. "Ode on a Grecian Urn" is also included in: Moss, Howard, ed. *Keats.* New York: Dell Publishing, 1959. Print.

Klinck, Carl F. *Wilfred Campbell: A Study in Late Provincial Victorianism.* Toronto: Ryerson Press, 1942. Print.

Klinck, Carl F., gen. ed., and Alfred G. Bailey, Claude Bissell, Roy Daniells, Northrop Frye, and Desmond Pacey, eds. *Literary History of Canada.* Toronto: University of Toronto Press, 1965. Print.

Lanier, Sidney. "The Marshes of Glynn." (This poem is part of Lanier's *Hymns of the Marshes*, an unfinished manuscript of lyrical nature poems.) It is included in: Williams, Oscar, ed. *The New Pocket Anthology of American Verse.* New York: Washington Square Press, 1955. pp. 249–253. Print.

Latham, David. "Charles Sangster." *The Oxford Companion to Canadian Literature.* Toronto: Oxford University Press, 1983. Print.

Lochhead, Douglas. "George Frederick Cameron." *The Oxford Companion to Canadian Literature.* Toronto: Oxford University Press, 1983. Print.

—. *High Marsh Road: Lines for a Diary.* Toronto: Anson-Cartwright Editions, 1980. Print.

—. *Weathers: Poems New and Selected.* Fredericton, New Brunswick: Goose Lane Editions, 2002. Print.

Lynch, Gerald, ed. *Bliss Carman: A Reappraisal.* Ottawa: University of Ottawa Press, 1990. Print.

Marsh, James H., ed. *The Canadian Encyclopedia.* Edmonton: Hurtig Publishers, 1985. Print.

Marshall, Tom. *Harsh and Lovely Land: The Major Canadian Poets and the Making of a Canadian Tradition.* Vancouver: University of British Columbia Press, 1979. Print.

Mayea, Amy. "Oh Canada, with not so Glowing Hearts, We See Thee Rise." *First Monday* June 2021. pp. 5 & 50. (Box 340, 395 Broadway Street, Wyoming, Ontario N0N 1T0) Print.

McLay, Catherine M., ed. *Canadian Literature: the beginnings to the 20th century.* Toronto: McClelland and Stewart, 1974. Print.

McMullen, Lorraine, ed. *The Lampman Symposium*. Ottawa: University of Ottawa Press, 1976. Print.

Mount, Nick. *When Canadian Literature Moved to New York*. Toronto: University of Toronto Press, 2005. Print.

Pomeroy, Elsie M. *Sir Charles G.D. Roberts: A Biography*. Toronto: Ryerson Press, 1943. Print.

Purdy, Al. *Beyond Remembering: The Collected Poems of Al Purdy*. Madeira Park, British Columbia: Harbour Publishing, 2000. Print.

—. *The Cariboo Horses*. Toronto: McClelland & Stewart, 1965. Print.

—. *The Enchanted Echo*. Vancouver: Clarke & Stuart, 1944. Print.

—. *To Paris Never Again*. Madeira Park, British Columbia: Harbour Publishing, 1997. Print.

Rittenhouse, Jessie B. *The Younger American Poets*. First published in 1904. Print. Facsimile edition by Forgotten Books (FB &c Ltd., Dalton House, 60 Windsor Avenue, London SW19 2RR, England). Print.

Ross, Malcolm. *The Impossible Sum of Our Traditions: Reflections on Canadian Literature*. Toronto: McClelland and Stewart, 1986. Print.

Shepard, Odell. *Bliss Carman*. Toronto: McClelland & Stewart, 1923. Print.

Smith, A.J.M., ed. *Masks of Poetry: Canadian Critics on Canadian Verse*. Toronto: McClelland & Stewart, 1962. Print.

Sosin, Jack M. *Whitehall and the Wilderness: The Middle West in British Colonial Policy, 1760-1775*. Westport, Connecticut: Greenwood Press, reprint edition, 1980. Print. (Original edition: Lincoln, Nebraska: University of Nebraska Press, 1961. Print.)

Souster, Raymond. *When We Are Young*. Montreal: First Statement, 1945. Print.

Souster, Raymond and Richard Woollatt, eds. *These loved, these hated lands*. Toronto: Doubleday Canada, 1975. Print.

Strong-Boag, Veronica and Carole Gerson. *Paddling Her Own Canoe: Times and Texts of E. Pauline Johnson (Tekahionwake)*. Toronto: University of Toronto Press, 2000. Print.

Tennyson, Alfred. *Idylls of the King*. London: Edward Moxon & Co., 1859. Print. An epilogue "To The Queen" was added in 1873. The True North is cited in this epilogue.

Thompson, John. *At the Edge of the Chopping There are No Secrets*. Toronto: House of Anansi, 1973. Print.

—. *I Dream Myself Into Being: Collected Poems*. Toronto: House of Anansi, 1991. Print.

Tierney, Frank M. "Charles Sangster." *Dictionary of Canadian Biography*, Volume XII (1891-1900). Toronto and Québec: University of Toronto and Université Laval, 1966.

Tierney, Frank M., ed. *The Isabella Valancy Crawford Symposium*. Ottawa: University of Ottawa Press, 1979. Print.

Toye, William, ed. *The Oxford Companion to Canadian Literature*. Toronto: Oxford University Press, 1983. Print.

Traill, Catharine Parr. *The Backwoods of Canada: Being Letters from the Wife of an Emigrant Officer, Illustrative of the Domestic Economy of British America*. London: Charles Knight, The Library of Entertaining Knowledge, 1836. Print.

The Truth and Reconciliation Commission of Canada. *Honouring the Truth, Reconciling for the Future: Summary of the Final Report of the Truth and Reconciliation Commission of Canada*. Winnipeg, 2015.

Untermeyer, Louis, ed. *Modern American Poetry: A Critical Anthology*. New York: Harcourt, Brace, 1919. Print. Facsimile edition by Forgotten Books (FB &c Ltd., Dalton House, 60 Windsor Avenue, London SW19 2RR, England). Print.

Whalen, Terry. *Bliss Carman and His Works*. Toronto: ECW Press, n.d. Print.

Woollatt, Richard and Raymond Souster, eds. *Sights and Sounds*. Toronto: Gage Publishing, 1973. Print.

Write. Volume 49, Number 2–Summer 2021. The Writers' Union of Canada. Print.

Wrong, George M. *Canada and the American Revolution*. Toronto: The Macmillan Company, 1935. Print.

Letters to the Author

Alexander, Becky D. Letter to the author. 10 May 2020.

Bowering, George. Letter to the author. 8 May 2020.

Briesmaster, Allan. Letter to the author. 9 May 2020.

Clarke, George Elliott. Letter to the author. 8 May 2020.

Eaton, Margaret Patricia. Two letters to the author. 8 May 2020.

Gervais, Marty. Letter to the author. 10 May 2020.

Gordon, Katherine L. "An Appreciation For Agnes Ethelwyn Wetherald." Unpublished article sent to the author on 4 March 2017.

Inman, Keith. Letter to the author. 9 May 2020.

Lee, John B. Letter to the author. 8 May 2020.

Marchand, Blaine. Letter to the author. 8 May 2020.

Meyer, Bruce. Letter to the author. 11 May 2020.

Moritz, A.F. Letter to the author. 11 May 2020.

Morton, Colin. Letter to the author. 8 May 2020.

Mutala, Marion. Letter to the author. 12 May 2020.

Rogers, Linda. Letter to the author. 9 May 2020.

Shenfeld, Karen. Letter to the author. 12 May 2020.

Wayman, Tom. Letter to the author. 8 May 2020.

Wolff, Elana. Letter to the author. 12 May 2020.

Index of Poems Presented in Full

Acknowledgements

It is with gratitude that I thank Ed Janzen and *Canadian Stories*. His journal published the chapters of this book, with the sole exception of my "Epilogue," always in a shortened form, between December 2016 and August 2021. I am grateful for the interest Ed and Susan Janzen have shown in my writing over the past several years.

I am indebted to Shona Deahl for her sharp eyes and keen wits displayed during her substantive edit of my manuscript, and for making sound suggestions and correcting my errors of omission, as well as for conducting important internet research. Thanks also to Al Moritz and Allan Briesmaster for reviewing an early draft of my manuscript, and to Terry Barker and Norma West Linder for proof-reading the text.

I express my appreciation for the research aid provided by Gary Miller and Terry Barker. And I also wish to acknowledge my debt to Dr. David Bentley, the Carl F. Klinck Professor of Canadian Literature at Western University, and his team at the *Canadian Poetry* journal for making long out-of-print books available via the internet and for his Canadian Poetry Project.

Finally, it is my deep pleasure to thank Michael Mirolla, Connie McParland, Elana Wolff, David Moratto, Julie Roorda, and the team at Guernica Editions for their faith in my writing, their excellent book design and editing, and for providing my beloved literary home, my safe harbour.

About the Author

James Deahl was born in Pittsburgh during 1945, and grew up in that city as well as in and around the Laurel Highlands of the Appalachian Mountains. He moved to Canada in 1970. For the past fifteen years he has been a full-time writer, editor, and translator. He is the author or editor of over thirty books (mostly poetry) and is the author of fifteen poetry chapbooks. His previous Guernica poetry collections are *Travelling The Lost Highway*, *Red Haws To Light The Field*, and *Rooms The Wind Makes*. A cycle of his poems is the focus of a one-hour television special, *Under The Watchful Eye*. (Both the video and an audiotape of this program have been reissued on DVD and CD by Silver Falls Video.) As a literary critic, Deahl has written about Milton Acorn, Raymond Souster, and Bruce Meyer, and he has lectured on Alden Nowlan, Robert Kroetsch, Canadian Postmodernism, and on the People's Poetry tradition.

The present study started life as a series of brief essays on the Confederation Poets for *Canadian Stories* as a way to celebrate Canada's Sesquicentennial in 2017. Somehow, these pieces grew into a book. Having spent time in Ottawa, Almonte, Sudbury, Wanup, Toronto, London, and Hamilton, James Deahl now lives in Sarnia, Ontario with his life partner, the novelist and poet Norma West Linder. He is the father of three daughters: Sarah, Simone, and Shona, with whom he is translating into English the selected poems of Émile Nelligan.